Deliver Us From Evil

Corruption and the Challenge to the Christian Faith and Church

Deliver Us From Evil

Corruption and the Challenge to the Christian Faith and Church

Roberto Laver

regnum
Mini Book Series

First published 2018 by Regnum Books International

Regnum is an imprint of the Oxford Centre for Mission Studies
St. Philip and St. James Church
Woodstock Road, Oxford OX2 6HR, UK
www.ocms.ac.uk/regnum

09 08 07 06 05 04 03 7 6 5 4 3 2 1

British Library Cataloguing in Publication Data. A catalogue record for this book is available from the British Library.

ISBN: 978-1-506475-52-3
eBook ISBN: 978-1-506475-53-0

Typeset in Candara by Words by Design.

Distributed by 1517 Media in the US and Canada

To Nora, my beloved wife
To Laura, Esteban and Larissa

Contents

Prologue

In September 2016, I participated in a conference with Christian leaders and representatives from Christian organizations around the world about the church and the global fight against corruption. About twenty of us came to the Oxford Centre for Mission Studies in England – all from diverse professional backgrounds, including academics, theologians, lawyers, medical professionals, social activists and leaders of NGOs. The majority of the group was directly involved in work that promoted public integrity and reduced corruption in their communities, both within the church and broadly in society. The next month, I attended the annual meetings of the International Monetary Fund (the Fund) and the World Bank in Washington, D.C. In a panel about corruption, the general counsel of the Fund expressed that the fight against corruption fundamentally requires the strengthening of values and norms of a society. For someone like me, who has worked with international organizations for the majority of my professional life, this was a true and surprising recognition. I could not stop thinking of that opportune Oxford meeting.

In many ways, the seeds for this book were planted more than two decades ago, at a time when I was working as a lawyer in the World

Bank. I was assigned to be a member of some of the first project teams addressing judicial reform in Latin America. These initiatives tried, among other things, to reduce judicial corruption in the region. My experience as a World Bank official in these projects was very stimulating intellectually. Justice was a totally new sector for the World Bank, and there was enormous potential to have a great impact on the societies most plagued by corruption. However, the experience was intensely frustrating. The challenge of judicial corruption, just as with corruption in general, required a holistic focus that exceeded the narrow scope and technocratic approach of the World Bank. The profound questions of social ethics and the fundamental role of cultural values and norms were not relevant, much less prioritized, by the World Bank. As we will see, the results speak for themselves.

This book is a product of a convergence of the diverse areas of law, international development and the integral mission of the Christian church. As a lawyer, academic and consultant in international development, I have had the opportunity to work extensively in the areas of governance, law and anti-corruption. I know, in theory and practice, the focuses, methods and tools that international development organizations use to fight corruption. I have seen at firsthand and endured the limitations of the mainstream approaches to combat corruption. Complementing this, my experience in global missions has allowed me to affirm, understand and appreciate the responsibility and great potential of the Christian church – as a community of believers – to be an agent of social transformation. I also fully recognize that we, as communities of believers, are falling short in modelling public integrity and playing an active protagonist role in the fight against corruption. This book will hopefully help believers and the church to reflect on, awaken to and engage with the profound injustice of corruption.

Introduction

An outspoken author observes of his nation that its leaders are contemptuous of justice – judges sell verdicts to the highest bidder while businesses pile up obscene wealth by cheating and fraud, as well as engage in shady deals and shifty scheming. He adds: "Everyone is trying to trap their brother. People are good at doing bad things with both hands. Officials ask for bribes. Judges take money to change their decisions in court. 'Important leaders' do whatever they want to do." And he warns everyone: "Don't trust your neighbour or trust a friend!"

This could be a fair description of many nations today. Yet, this author is the ancient prophet Micah speaking about Judah and Israel almost 2,500 years ago. Micah lived in a time when wealth and power were concentrated in the hands of a corrupt elite. These leaders abused their entrusted power for personal profit rather than for public service. They oppressed the less fortunate, exacerbating social inequality and undermining the foundations of a just society. Corruption had spread beyond the political and religious establishment – dishonesty was so pervasive that it was impossible to trust anyone.

Corruption scandals are daily news in most places. Recent polls show corruption to be the most serious problem and the most talked about topic worldwide. Over half the global population believes that corruption has become worse and that national governments are handling the fight against corruption poorly. Powerful groups, rather than the public good, are judged to be driving government actions. About one third of those polled think their government is largely or entirely run by groups acting in their own interests rather than for the benefit of the citizens. This is more than just paying bribes: almost two out of three people believe that personal contacts and relationships help to get things done in the public sector.

Corruption inflicts huge costs on societies and human flourishing. It is damaging to equity and fairness as well as to economic performance and the welfare of society. Countless studies and econometric estimates show that corruption has devastating effects on the political, social and economic development of communities and countries. The negative effects of corruption directly counter the work of the church, which seeks to spread God's *shalom* in the world. The economic and social impacts of corruption on the poor have been widely documented both by secular and Christian agencies, which should catch the attention of the church and drive it to action.

Today, reducing corruption is centre-stage on the global agenda. Anti-corruption efforts are considered essential to helping poor people escape poverty and countries achieve sustainable development. States have signed treaties and enacted laws to prevent, control and penalize corruption, while many have established special anti-corruption agencies. The business sector places greater emphasis on corporate governance and ethics, and multinational companies have formed several different coalitions to fight corruption. Civil society groups, most notably Transparency International, have emerged to build greater awareness and act as advocates and watchdogs. These developments have been accompanied by a growing output from the academic community; and the fight against corruption has emerged as a central element of the work of international development agencies in supporting political and economic development.

Despite greater global awareness and decades of reforms, the cancer of corruption is not receding. Most countries, as evidenced by corruption measures, can't seem to find a way out of the corruption trap. Reforms promoted by the international community are not producing the desired results. These reforms are largely driven by a technocratic and economic approach. They have mostly focused on formal structures, rules and mechanisms of transparency and accountability. In the face of the failure of these interventions, there is a growing recognition that corruption will not be reduced unless we drive out the underlying cultures that enable and foster this cancer.

Corruption is not only a problem that affects a particular group, sector or institution. It exists everywhere, not only in poor and developing countries. In some countries, it is more exceptional and reduced in scope, while in others it is highly pervasive and endemic. While corruption is a complex and multi-causal phenomenon, it is in many ways a cultural problem in societies that validate and legitimize certain patterns of dysfunctional behaviour towards the public interest and the common good. To a large extent, politicians simply repeat and reflect attitudes and patterns of behaviour that society validates in other domains of human activity; it should not be surprising that, when they arrive in power, politicians and leaders do not change their behaviour. This is a problem and a challenge that involves us all.

Indeed, many forms of corruption are largely tolerated – or even legitimized and accepted – in many societies to the extent that they constitute normal behaviour. In my own region of Latin America, as in many other places, loyalty to family and friends often prevails over principles of justice and impartiality. People often look for 'levers' to gain advantages or privileges, or to avoid payment or punishment – to the detriment of what our neighbours and community deserve. People expect special treatment from members of their inner circle or 'tribe', informally pressuring and sanctioning those who do not act according to expectations. These attitudes towards favouritism, nepotism and undue influence reflect social norms, generally in conflict with formal norms that prescribe impartiality and integrity.

No matter how much institutional and legal engineering is attempted, corruption will not be reduced while underlying social norms remain unchallenged. One notices the substantial institutional reform in the public sector of developing and emerging countries over the last three decades or so. These nations have enacted laws for more professional and merit-based public service in areas of public employment, administrative procedures and public contracting. Also, new supervisory and oversight structures have been created, such as anti-corruption agencies and offices of ombudsmen. Despite all these legislative and institutional advances, the public sector in these societies continues to operate by social norms of favouritism, influence-peddling and impunity. Without a cultural transformation, the tide of corruption will not shift.

While the fight against corruption is central to the global agenda, it has not received the same attention and prominence by the church and its leaders, despite its profound social justice and ethical dimensions. Corruption is a subject of incredible relevance to the Christian faith, the integral mission of the church and to each believer. A corrupt society is a society that is lacking in solidarity and love for one's neighbour, in particular for those who suffer the most from this social cancer – the poor and marginalized who lie beyond the circles of power, influence and favouritism. God commands us to act with impartiality and without favouritism, and that we use honest 'weights and measures'. Many of our nations and societies today, with Christian majorities, resemble the Israel and Judah of the times of Micah. These are societies with low inter-personal trust, where favouritism, privilege and preferential treatment inform and shape relationships among citizens and between citizens and their government representatives. The fight against corruption is more than a political or economic issue. Public integrity is a virtue, an ethic of social living that allows for the equitable development of society and the realization of each individual's potential. This is the message of Micah and other prophets of the Old Testament.

The international community is waking up to the reality that corruption's solution lies beyond political and institutional reform. Deep cultural and ethical changes, as well as leaders who are models of integrity, are needed. We must then ask ourselves: 'What is the role of the church and its leaders? Which are the challenges and opportunities for promoting public integrity? How can we commit to achieving a society with greater integrity?'

This book speaks to the problem of corruption, particularly in countries where it is endemic and where the need to find new solutions to this social challenge is great. Its key message is one that is mostly neglected and marginalized by the international development community: corruption is also a cultural phenomenon, and the church offers – not without its own challenges – a high-potential alternative avenue for helping renovate cultural values and norms.

The academic literature that discusses corruption is abundant and growing every day. Research emerges from all disciplines, although economists dominate the studies of corruption. However, there is a lack of work about the potential role of the church. This book intends to provide a response to that gap and to catalyze dialogue about the role of faith and the church on the subject. This is not a book on the theology of governance or corruption. Instead, it is a book that, founded on thorough analysis of the global agenda on anti-corruption, argues that the church and all believers have the responsibility and potential to help transform corrupt societies – something that traditional reforms have not achieved.

This book is for a wide range of readers, including church and institutional leaders, members of missions organizations focused on humanitarian or development work, Christian NGO leaders, professionals in the public sector at international, national or local levels, and businesspeople in the private sector who deal with issues of governance and anti-corruption in their daily lives, as well as academics, activists and all those interested and concerned about the problem of corruption and seeking solutions.

This book is a reduced version of a previous book published by the author in Spanish and entitled: *Líbranos del Mal: La Corrupción y el Desafío para la Fe y la Iglesia Cristiana en América Latina*. Although many details and nuances from the original book are lost in this shortened form, the core message remains intact. The book is divided into two major parts: the problem of corruption and the solution to corruption. The first part – including Chapters One and Two – deals with the concept and the costs of corruption. The second part – Chapters Three, Four, Five and Six – discusses the prevailing anti-corruption strategies and programmes in the international community, the cultural dimension of corruption, and the role of faith and the church in fighting corruption.

Note

The endnotes list publications referred to in each chapter. More complete details can be found in Roberto Laver, *Líbranos del mal: la corrupción y el desafío para la fe y la iglesia cristiana en América Latina* (Oxford: Regnum, 2018).

The endorsements used on the rear cover of this book are also adapted from the endorsements for *Líbranos del mal.*

1. Defining Corruption

What is corruption? In facing this question, many believers might respond that it means all sin, perversion and evil. The first instance of the word in the Bible is used to describe the people in the time of the Flood; in other translations of the Bible, words such as 'evil' and 'ruined' are used instead of 'corrupt'. The word 'corruption' in the Hebrew and the Greek which are used in the Old and New Testaments respectively, alludes to destruction, decomposition or ruin. Although Scripture does not use the word 'corruption' in the sense of the specific political, economic and social phenomenon referred to here, it does not mean it has nothing to offer. In fact, the Scriptures have a lot to say about this particular notion of corruption. This is the corruption that is denounced by diverse voices in the Christian church, including Pope Francis, the World Council of Churches and the World Evangelical Alliance.

While corruption is not a new phenomenon in history, there is no uniform definition of it. Thousands of pages have been written about this question, and today it continues to be a permanent topic of reflection and debate. Eric Uslaner, Professor at the University of Maryland and one of the most recognized scholars on the subject, describes corruption as an 'elusive concept'. Even the United Nations Convention Against Corruption does not define the phenomenon, but instead simply typifies the various forms that it takes, such as money laundering, misappropriation of public funds or bribery. It is difficult to reach a full consensus on a definition, because what a society calls 'corrupt' will depend on its legislation, its codes of ethical conduct, its political system and public opinion.

Transparency International provides the most widely used definition of corruption: 'the abuse of entrusted power for private gain'. Although this definition has limitations, it recognizes that corruption is not limited to the public sector but extends to the private arena, including businesses and non-profit organizations.

I would argue that corruption should be understood as a misuse of power, authority or public resources, or a breach of public trust in a broad sense and with a profound moral dimension – not purely legalistic, technocratic or conditioned by cultural relativism. Corruption implies a fundamental distinction between private interests and the common good, whereby the private concern prevails and undermines the public one. In essence, corruption entails a tension – a conflict – between private and public interests.

A broader definition of corruption reminds us that it is much more than bribery. In most societies, corruption is systemic – it is not rare or isolated. Instead, corruption is pervasive and entrenched because, while formal laws and institutions of accountability to deter and punish corruption exist, their enforcement is absent, ineffective or weak. Public officials abuse power because they are neither deterred nor controlled by state-based accountability institutions or non-state accountability actors. The term 'corruption' is usually associated with high-level, grand bribery or embezzlement among politicians and businesses – these are the cases that make the headlines. However, corruption is much more than that and takes many different forms. Common to all corruption practices is a violation of trust, an undermining of the common good or interests of the community or society. Each and every form represents abuses of power, trust or authority for private gain, but differs in the particular characteristics of each case.

Bribery is one of the most widely recognized forms of corruption. For example, there is the case of the Swedish telecommunications firm, Telia Company AB, that allegedly paid bribes to facilitate its expansion in the Uzbek market and in 2017 was charged with the highest penalty to date by the US government for violations of its foreign corrupt practices law. Other forms include influence peddling, money laundering and embezzlement.

Influence peddling is when someone uses their influence in government or connections with persons in authority to obtain favours or preferential treatment for another person. This can be seen in the case of the appointment of the daughter of a minister in Argentina to the position of director at the Argentine central bank for which she did not meet the legal requirements.

An example of money laundering comes from Honduras, where purchases of overvalued medicines provide a way for wealthy, well-connected individuals to make illegally sourced income appear to be legitimate.

Embezzlement is when an individual holding office illegally uses public goods or funds for their personal enrichment, as was the case in 2016 with a Malaysian sovereign wealth fund. It was alleged that more than 3.5 billion USD in assets were misappropriated by high-level officials and associates managing the fund, part of which was found in former Malaysian Prime Minister Najib Razak's bank accounts in 2018.

Measuring Corruption

The most widely used measure of corruption is Transparency International's Corruption Perception Index (CPI). Since the early 1990s, Transparency International has issued the CPI on an annual basis. While not a perfect instrument, the CPI offers a snapshot of national levels of perceived corruption in the public sector. Every

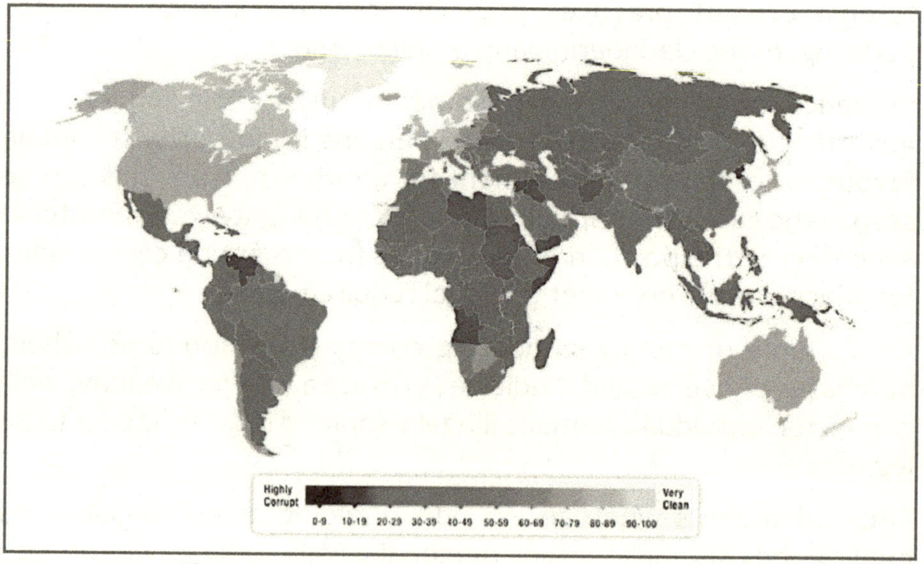

Figure 1: Corruption Perceptions Index 2017

Rank	Country	Score	Rank	Country	Score
1	New Zealand	89	161	Cambodia	21
2	Denmark	88	161	Congo	21
3	Finland	85	161	Democratic Republic of the Congo	21
3	Norway	85	161	Tajikistan	21
3	Switzerland	85	165	Chad	20
6	Singapore	84	165	Eritrea	20
6	Sweden	84	167	Angola	19
8	Canada	82	167	Turkmenistan	19
8	Luxembourg	82	169	Iraq	18
8	Netherlands	82	169	Venezuela	18
8	United Kingdom	82	171	Korea, North	17
12	Germany	81	171	Equatorial Guinea	17
13	Australia	77	171	Guinea Bissau	17
13	Hong Kong	77	171	Libya	17
13	Iceland	77	175	Sudan	16
16	Austria	75	175	Yemen	16
16	Belgium	75	177	Afghanistan	15
16	United States of America	75	178	Syria	14
19	Ireland	74	179	South Sudan	12
20	Japan	73	180	Somalia	9

Table 1: Corruption Perceptions Index 2017: Ranking of top and bottom twenty countries

year, the CPI's best performers rarely vary. Six countries have always ranked in the top ten positions – Denmark, New Zealand, Finland, Sweden, the Netherlands and Singapore. The vast majority of nations, however, remain virtually locked in a vicious cycle of relatively high and widespread corruption. The global results of the CPI can be seen in Figure 1 and Table 1, with more details on Christianity, perceived corruption and the amount of foreign aid to a country provided in *Appendix 1: Selected Country Data*.

2. The Costs of Corruption

Corruption is an insidious plague that has a wide range of corrosive effects on societies. It undermines democracy and the rule of law, leads to violations of human rights, distorts markets, erodes the quality of life, and allows organized crime, terrorism and other threats to human security to flourish.

– Kofi Annan, former
Secretary-General of the United Nations

The most comprehensive studies report the direct annual cost of corruption is approximately one trillion USD. In contrast, foreign aid (flows of official financing given globally) amounts to 142.6 billion USD. The cost of corruption in Africa alone is estimated at 148 billion USD a year, 25% of the continent's gross domestic product (GDP) and about 300% of the foreign aid it receives. These figures approximate the waste of financial resources misdirected because of bribes and stolen public funds; yet the full costs of corruption are much higher than this. There are arguably no economic estimates that can fully capture the real damage of corruption on societies and their members. How does one calculate the losses for a society where children and youth come to believe that personal effort and merit do not count, and that success comes through cheating, favouritism and bribery? It is impossible to quantify the price society pays for the indirect web of impact that corruption has on society in its many forms: impunity, influence peddling, nepotism, embezzlement, bribery, extortion – and more.

Corruption has devastating effects for the social, political and economic development of nations. Corruption inhibits economic development through lower investment and productivity. Experts estimate that a worsening of one point in the CPI scale would entail a reduction in productivity of four percentage points in GDP, while a six-point improvement in the CPI would imply approximately 20% growth in GDP.

Along with the United Nations and other international organizations, Christian leaders and institutions have increasingly recognized the devastating effects of corruption. In 2006, in a conference conducted in the Vatican about the fight against corruption, the Catholic Church, through its Pontifical Council for Justice and Peace, recognized the gravity of corruption and its effects when referring to it as an act that is 'a very serious fact that distorts the political system'. The conference note went on to say: "Corruption causes serious harm from a material point of view and places a costly burden on economic growth; still more harmful are its effects on immaterial goods, closely connected to the qualitative and human dimension of life in society." The World Evangelical Alliance and the Micah Network, in the launch of 'Exposed', a global campaign against corruption, recognized the negative consequences in all aspects of development.

The Cost to Human Development

Although the full range of adverse impacts is difficult to track, we can see the effect of corruption by zooming into particular cases. Investigators of the magnitude 7.0 earthquake on 12 January 2010 in Haiti reported that the combination of the size of the earthquake and the widespread corruption throughout the country was responsible for such a devastating impact: 100,000 to 300,000 deaths and 1.3 million people left homeless. In contrast, just seven weeks later, a magnitude 8.8 earthquake (500 times more powerful than the earthquake in Haiti) hit two port cities in Chile. However, less than 500 people died and the material damages were minimal. Though there were certainly differences between the two cities' epicentre location, population density and type of earthquake, corruption in Haiti surely had an effect. The use of low-quality building materials and limited public access to construction equipment and medical supplies were, in many cases, directly linked to bribes and the misappropriation of public funds. In 2010, Haiti's Corruption Perceptions Index was 2.2/10 and Chile was 7.2/10. Estimates show that, over the past thirty years, 83% of deaths connected with earthquake-related building collapses took place in countries with endemic corruption.

Country-specific research confirms that corruption has measurable local impacts on specific health and education outcomes. A Philippine-specific study showed that corruption decreased immunization rates and national test score levels, increased national test score variation and even measurably increased wait times at hospitals. Research in Tanzania found that the health workers created artificial shortages and deliberately lowered the quality of service in order to extract higher payments from patients, or increased their leverage in bargaining, which led to more expensive and lower-quality health care, as well as inducing non-corrupt health workers to reduce their quality of care.

A global econometric study found that a single one-point decrease in the CPI (indexed from 0 to 100) is associated with about a 10% decrease in secondary school enrolment rates (for scale, on the CPI 2017, Norway scored 85, United States scored 75, Bahamas scored 65 and Rwanda scored 55). Another study found that 1.6% of all deaths of children under five can be indirectly attributed to corruption. This means 140,000 children die because of corruption, compared with the familiar killers of malaria (306,371 deaths of children under five), HIV/AIDS (986,724 deaths) and measles (73,848 deaths). These econometric studies are but a few quantitative evidences of the diverse and deep effects of corruption on society.

The Cost to the Poor

Tragically, the poor and marginalized suffer the worst consequences of corruption. The World Bank affirms that corruption is 'the greatest obstacle to reducing poverty'. Corruption affects poverty by slowing economic growth, exacerbating the poverty and inequality already present. Likewise, corruption deepens poverty through its negative effect on governance of weakening institutions, reducing citizen participation and reducing the quality of public services and infrastructure.

The poor suffer from less accessible public services, which are not only lower quality, but also more expensive than what is accessible to the rest of society. The poor struggle daily against the pressure to pay bribes to access basic public services like hospitals, medicine and public infrastructure. Corruption directly extracts money from the poor because they are powerless against the pressure. Poor people pay larger shares of their income in bribes than richer people and are specifically discriminated against in their access to public services. A leader of the evangelical Christian NGO Tearfund shares: "We know from our work in Africa, Asia, and Latin America that it is the poorest and most vulnerable people who suffer the most as a result of bribery." Worse, the poor are denied public help, such as housing or subsidized credit, because those benefits are illegitimately assigned to people with greater leverage. Facing a situation in which the public service is of a lower quality, the poor opt for even more expensive private options.

Corruption undoes and prevents all forms of development that are for the benefit of the poor. Resources intended for the poor, including foreign aid, do not reach the people that need it, but are diverted to enrich corrupt elites. Diversion of funds, unfair preferential contracting, money laundering, extortion – all forms of corruption – stifle global development from the start. Additionally, whatever public money is spent for public use in countries with higher levels of corruption, public spending tends to be directed towards infrastructure or the military rather than health or education, which would directly benefit the poor. These projects are riddled with fraud, making them more expensive, and pulling even more money away from social programmes. It is no wonder that Transparency International writes: "The poor, whether in developing or highly industrialized countries, are the most penalized by corruption. They are also more pessimistic about the prospects for less corruption in the future." If we want to build stronger health, education, business, trade or government systems, we must simultaneously support anti-corruption efforts to fully address the roots of poverty.

Corruption aggravates poverty and inequality by selectively oppressing the poor, as seen in Nepal where a government official refused on multiple occasions to process a farmer's application for a government subsidy unless he was paid a bribe. Corruption also reduces social cohesion and trust by weakening the rule of law and increasing violation of human rights. Take, for example, an employee in Croatia brought forth a minor court case for his unfair dismissal and was dragged through the process without an outcome for eleven years until an international NGO became involved and the case was won in a single month. Corruption increases conflict and insecurity by weakening the rule of law. This is clearly seen in a case in Venezuela where the identification cards of people in makeshift settlements were confiscated by police officers who then demanded bribes for the return of the cards. The people feared their identification cards would be dropped at a crime scene if they refused to hand over the money. With no exaggeration, corruption can be an issue of life and death.

Fortunately, many voices from the church have expressed their focus on protecting the poor from corruption. In 2013, the Secretary General of the World Council of Churches, Dr Olav Fykse Tviet, declared that the preferential option for the poor is foundational to the mission of the church's fight against corruption. In 2014, the Secretary General of the World Evangelical Alliance, Dr Geoff Tunnicliffe, maintained that the care of the poor is a central Biblical mandate and, consequently, corruption is a priority for the church.

The Pontifical Council of Justice and Peace declares that corruption threatens the principles of the social doctrine of the Catholic Church, including the preferential option for the poor.

The Cost to the Church

Corruption undermines church efforts for relief and development; the church's response to Scripture's call towards justice, peace and care for the poor is stopped in its tracks. The church assists poor communities worldwide through education, health, agricultural, micro-finance and other poverty alleviation programmes. These efforts, however, are adversely affected by corrupt practices that are endemic and pervasive in poor communities. This may take the form of financial corruption, such as bribery and the embezzlement of funds, or other non-financial forms such as the unfair use and allocation of resources and opportunities through in-group favouritism and nepotism.

Even more importantly, corruption damages the credibility of the church. Cases of embezzlement of church resources and/or bribes being paid to cover up sexual abuse are unfortunately familiar headlines in the news. These stories shatter the credibility of any message of integrity, honesty, justice or love that is preached. These cases of corruption act as accusers of the church's failure and put it on public display.

3. The Anti-Corruption Reform Agenda

> *The experience of public-sector reform mandated by international aid agencies for developing countries at the turn of the twenty-first century demonstrates the futility of a purely technical approach.*
>
> *– Francis Fukuyama*

Since the 1990s, there has been an explosion of efforts to combat corruption, particularly in developing and emerging countries, due to the global consensus that addressing corruption and building good governance is essential for societal progress and development. Virtually all such countries have implemented anti-corruption reforms with the technical and financial assistance of international aid agencies, which have invested billions of dollars in such reforms. These agencies include those known as multilateral (i.e. the World Bank) and bilateral (i.e. the United States Agency for International Development and the UK's Department for International Development).

The World Bank (hereafter, the Bank) has led anti-corruption efforts among international aid agencies. In 1997, the Bank issued its first anti-corruption strategy. The strategy drew on previous conceptual works (notably the Bank's 1992 and 1994 pieces on governance) and operational experience in public sector reform and private sector development. Following the Bank's lead, the Organisation for Economic Co-operation and Development, the United Nations and several multilateral and bilateral aid agencies placed anti-corruption high on their development agendas and developed their own strategies and programmes. What are these anti-corruption reforms about? What is their logic and rationale? What are their results?

The Nature of the Reforms

The anti-corruption reforms, at their core, have been about strengthening institutions in the public sector. International aid agencies argue that corruption is a 'manifestation of institutional failures', and that it 'tends to flourish when institutions are weak'. What are these institutional failures and weaknesses? Basically, institutional failures are when politicians and civil servants hold too much power and discretion, transparency of government is weak and the mechanisms of accountability are deficient. To curb corrupt behaviour, these institutional reforms aim at increasing the costs and reducing opportunities for corruption in the public sector. This is generally done by changes in structures (i.e. creating a new anti-corruption agency or enhancing the technical capacity of existing organizations), laws (i.e. new laws on disclosure of information, corporate governance, protection of whistle-blowers), and policies and procedures (i.e. reducing government subsidies and regulations, salary increases for public officials, new and more transparent budgetary and procurement processes).

The institutional reforms can be categorized into two types: 'supply-side' and 'demand-side'.

The supply-side interventions are focused on those who 'supply governance': government agencies and public servants. They involve two kinds of interventions: those that seek to improve the management of finances and human resources (i.e. rules to hire public servants on the basis of merit or make the budget process more transparent), and those that seek to strengthen oversight and controls (i.e. creating a new anti-corruption agency).

As a complement to the supply-side interventions, the demand-side ones emerged in an attempt to improve the targeting of endemic corruption. There was a realization that change in governance was not going to happen just by focusing on government and public servants; reforms also needed to focus on individuals and organizations beyond government by empowering them to demand accountability from their government representatives and by promoting better governance in the business sector. Three kinds of demand-side interventions emerged: those that increased opportunities for participation in and oversight of the government by NGOs, the media and citizens in general (i.e. disclosure of personal assets by politicians); those that made the private sector, corporations and their leaders, more competitive and responsible; and those that sought to promote transparency and participation in the political process (i.e. rules on political campaign finance).

In practice, these supply and demand reforms adopt the view that corruption is largely an accountability problem. The premise is that the accountability relationships are weak horizontally – between politicians and bureaucrats, as well as vertically – between the electorate and politicians. This view drives anti-corruption reforms to focus on oversight, control and penalizing political leaders and bureaucrats. The supply and demand reforms thus largely focus on horizontal accountability and vertical accountability, respectively.

Horizontal accountability reforms have focused on increasing transparency and accountability mechanisms within the state apparatus, including audit agencies, anti-corruption agencies, the judiciary and other formal oversight agencies and processes.

To complement efforts to improve horizontal accountability within the state, international aid agencies turned their attention to vertical accountability between the state and its people. At one level, reforms support 'democratic accountability' – that is, more transparency and participation in the political process (i.e. changes in electoral rules, political competition and political campaign finance). At another level, reforms support 'societal accountability' through improvements in the monitoring of public officials by civil society and the media (i.e. laws on the right to information).

Results of the Reforms

While international development actors have brought corruption concerns to the fore, and advances have been made, the results of the anti-corruption reforms have been very disappointing – particularly in addressing systemic corruption. Indeed, there is a greater awareness of the problem worldwide. Countries have greater access to a diverse set of technical, legal, institutional and administrative tools to combat it, and there are better measurement indexes. New international treaties have been signed and new actors have emerged to fight it. There have been cases where high-level politicians and business leaders have been convicted and imprisoned. However, the 'cancer of corruption' is not receding.

Top expert analysts admit that most countries are at least as corrupt today as they were before anti-corruption reforms. Indeed 'according to all available measures, in most countries that were plagued by widespread corruption before the reforms were initiated, corruption remains rampant even today'. International aid agencies admit the failure of the reforms in their own evaluations. In its latest evaluation in 2011 (including fifty country programmes and 200 operations), the Bank 'found no cases where Bank programs effectively addressed systemic corruption or deep-seated governance pathologies (such as the distribution of public goods on the basis of loyalty)'. In a separate review, six international donor agencies found that, although their projects strengthened formal systems and institutions, this did not translate into a reduction of corruption. In fact, 'there is little evidence to show that donor success in strengthening country institutions and systems has contributed to increased domestic accountability, and encouraging associated behavioural changes or cultural shift, at national level'. Many other evaluations of anti-corruption reforms by international development agencies reached a similar conclusion – that anti-corruption initiatives have not been effective.

> *Institutions come and go, but corruption persists…*
>
> *– Eric M. Uslaner*

Such disappointing results lead one to wonder what else is needed to get at the heart of corruption. While there may be several factors, a big reason for the disappointing results lies in how the problem is understood and approached. The reforms have largely dealt with the symptoms of weak institutions, but not the underlying causes. They focus on formal mechanisms and tools while neglecting the broader context, including the political culture in which such tools and mechanisms unfold. The approach is characterized as largely technocratic – corruption is reduced to a set of technical challenges that require technical solutions. It is an approach that '[overemphasizes] tools to the detriment of analysis of context' and overlooks 'the fact that anti-corruption reform, though it has important technical aspects, also is a social and political phenomenon driven by human behaviour and local circumstances'.

Before implementing anti-corruption reform, it is essential to understand the socio-political context and how it may limit the efficacy of the interventions. In the absence of a good analysis of the context in which the interventions will operate, the preconditions for success are not properly identified and addressed. Thus it is imperative 'to investigate the extent to which pre-existing social contexts "enable" or "disable" the intended mechanisms of change.'

When we talk about context, we inevitably deal with culture in the form of the prevailing values and attitudes in a society. The institutional reforms are mediated and conditioned by culture. And cultural values and attitudes might be significant 'disabling' factors of the intended institutional reforms to strengthen transparency and accountability. Yet, cultural factors are not adequately addressed in anti-corruption reforms – they are blind spots.

Indeed, these 'cultural' blind spots cut across supply-side and demand-side approaches. Supply-side reforms mistakenly assume that political leaders are willing, committed and dependable partners in promoting fair and honest government. It is simply a question of adopting new laws, processes, mechanisms and other formal tools to prevent, detect and sanction the corrupt behaviour of bureaucrats. However, as evidenced by the evaluations of reforms, given the lack of legitimacy and commitment of political leaders and elites, corruption persists.

The demand-side interventions to build civil activism are also subject to mistaken assumptions about the underlying values and attitudes of civil society in general. The demand-side approach generally assumes that civil society organizations and ordinary citizens are a benevolent and homogenous group that needs more access to information, awareness of its rights and empowerment tools. If ordinary citizens are provided information and accountability mechanisms to make a stand, the belief is that corruption will automatically be curbed.

There is no doubt that greater awareness and social accountability mechanisms are extremely necessary and important; however, the demand-side interventions 'neglect to assess the ways in which civil society organizations depend on other factors and actors in their efforts to create change'. The initiatives to promote civil activism must take into account, among other things, cultural factors such as interpersonal trust, public honesty, particularistic relationships, expectation of favouritism and preference.

Demand-side reforms often include the creation of mechanisms and opportunities for the social monitoring of public services such as education and health. These reforms assume that a more informed public will lead to greater empowerment and better control over corruption. However, empirical assessments of such interventions demonstrate that one cannot simply assume that citizens will automatically fight corruption. They may well be participants in, and beneficiaries of, corrupt acts. Citizens may also fear the consequences of denouncing the corruption of powerful public officials, or they may believe that the problem is too complex and any efforts to counter it are futile.

Transparency and accountability initiatives, in and of themselves, represent technocratic exercises that can easily be manipulated or neutralized by dishonest governments. NGOs may well be too embedded in the same patterns of systemic corruption affecting politicians and bureaucrats. They might be lacking, or perceived as lacking, legitimacy or commitment. In fact, 'in a country where corruption is widespread and endemic, one can question how easy it is to find NGOs that are clean'.

Further, we cannot assume that citizens will automatically be interested in denouncing corruption even if strong political and bureaucratic accountability mechanisms exist. Awareness and empowerment do not *automatically* translate into reduced corruption. It is not simply a question of putting citizens in control of their political leaders. Citizens who are tolerant of corruption, or certain types of corruption, will not enforce accountability mechanisms. If there exists a political culture of pervasive acceptance and tolerance of corruption or some of its expressions, it is not surprising that accountability mechanisms, while progressive and attractive on paper, are ineffective.

4. Corruption and Culture

For my friends everything, for my enemies the law.

– credited to several presidents in Latin America

Corruption and culture, on their own, are extremely complex phenomena. When talking about culture, we mean the values, attitudes, beliefs and underlying presuppositions that prevail among individuals in a society. It is worth emphasizing that culture is only one driving factor – though a critical one – among many factors that influence corruption.

As seen in the previous chapter, anti-corruption reforms focus primarily on institutional incentives and mechanisms to counter corruption. Until very recently, cultural factors received virtually no attention in anti-corruption discourse and practice. Perhaps, given the limited success of the anti-corruption reform agenda, there has been a renewed interest regarding the relationship between culture and corruption. Though 'institutional engineering' studies still dominate the academic landscape, an emerging series of works examines the relationship between culture and corruption from different perspectives. This emerging literature, however, has not had any substantial impact on diagnostic work and anti-corruption interventions by international aid agencies. Drawing from the emerging literature, this chapter attempts to outline significant findings and insights on culture and corruption that help us better understand the factors behind the limited impact of institutional reforms. This does not pretend to be an all-exhaustive review of the relationship between culture and corruption, if that were ever possible. This chapter does not draw any final and categorical judgements, but instead seeks to highlight several entry points into the culture–corruption conversation. Culture is not an easy subject to deal with and there is always the danger of drawing generalizations and oversimplifications. At the same time, there is the risk that, for political correctness or otherwise, the factor of culture is minimized, blinding us to the real force and influence of culture on corrupt behaviour.

Culture as an Independent Factor

At the World Bank of the 1990s, the notion of culture as a key factor of corruption was considered a myth by some, who pointed to the results of a 'natural experiment' carried out with public officials and ordinary citizens in developing countries. In the survey, respondents were asked how they would react if, in a parking lot at night, they found an envelope containing 2,000 USD: would they return the envelope to the police or would they keep it? After this, they were asked the same question again, with the variation that this time there is a 30% probability that they would be monitored by a hidden video camera. These World Bank officials found the results of the survey to be quite startling, taking it as proof that monitoring and control play a key role in controlling or fostering corruption. In the first case – with no chance of being caught – the majority of the respondents would either keep the money or take it home to think about it. In the second case, with a 30% possibility of being monitored, the result was reversed so that the majority would immediately return the money.

It is difficult to see how this experiment would rule out culture as a contributing factor of corruption. The experiment does not deal with an abuse of power, authority or public trust for private gain, but rather an illegal appropriation by a private individual of private monies. Further, it shows a change of behaviour due to the higher probability of control, but does not acknowledge that the effectiveness of the control itself (that an actual sanction would be applied) is highly related to the social acceptance of the act in question. If a certain corrupt practice – for example, favouritism, nepotism or influence peddling – is socially acceptable, one wonders how effective control mechanisms of such behaviour would be. The experiment also assumes the honesty and effective control of the police. Yet, this is where the problem may reside.

Fortunately, there is more relevant and helpful data to draw upon. Economists Raymond Fisman and Edward Miguel studied a fascinating 'natural experiment' in order to shed light on this enigmatic nexus between culture and corruption. They examined illegal parking by diplomats from 149 countries posted to the United Nations Headquarters in New York City between 1998 and 2002. Before 2002, these diplomats were not subject to sanctions for breaking parking rules: if a diplomat illegally parked his/her car in New York City and received a fine, it could not be enforced. This meant that all the diplomats, who were the subjects of the study, were under the same institutional incentives of zero enforcement.

One hundred and fifty thousand (150,000) unpaid fines by diplomats are estimated to have accumulated between November 1997 and the end of 2002. Following traditional economic models, one would expect that the diplomats, whatever their country of origin, would exhibit similar behaviour in view of their immunity.

Fisman and Miguel tested this hypothesis and reached some very revealing conclusions: they found a strong and positive correlation between the number of unpaid fines by diplomats and the level of corruption in their country of origin. Diplomats from countries with higher corruption levels had a greater number of unpaid fines, while diplomats from countries with lower levels of corruption had either no unpaid fines or very few compared with their colleagues. These findings go against the predictions of standard economic models of crime in situations of zero enforcement. The standard model would predict that the level of unpaid fines would be high for all diplomats and similar across the board. However, the study showed that diplomats from countries with lower levels of corruption (e.g. Norway) complied with the rules regardless of sanctions; while those from highly corrupt nations (e.g. Nigeria) breached the rules. The study suggests that cultural or social norms related to corruption appear to be deeply engrained and played a key role in the decisions of government officials concerning corruption.

Cultures of Corruption: Internalized, Socially Accepted and Promoted

The UN diplomats in the above study mostly came from societies where abuse of authority, power and public trust is, to a large extent, the norm, not the exception. These were not isolated examples of behaviour, exclusive to one particular group, sector or institution in society, but rather was widespread in all sectors and social levels. Generally, it is not in the absence of laws prohibiting such practices that such behaviour occurs, but it is rather in spite of such laws. The problem is not a lack of adequate laws, but the prevalence of informal norms that diverge and conflict with such laws.

These informal norms of corruption reflect, in a sense, a weak commitment to the common or public good. The World Bank points out that societies with endemic corruption share certain characteristics. One is that the notion of public interest is not engrained and shared among members of society; while another characteristic is that favoured stakeholder groups see the state as an extension of private interests. These societies believe laws apply to some but not to others, and when the law is used, it is to further private interests rather than protect the public interest. Another characteristic is that merit is not important in public service, and personal or political relationships prevail in public contracts. Finally, there is weak accountability as long as impunity prevails in these societies.

These corruption norms or patterns of behaviour are not simply an outgrowth of weak political structures and bad economic incentives but also, and more importantly, are driven by the prevailing social values, attitudes and expectations of the local culture. Expert observers from a wide range of regions and countries talk about a 'culture of corruption' in reference to the values, attitudes and expectations in their respective societies.

Indeed, there are certain cultural traits associated with corruption. Many societies uphold cultural values that clash with good governance and fairness. Latin America generally demonstrates a case of how one particular form of corruption has been integrated into the fabric of society: favouritism. Of course, instances of favouritism occur in all parts of the globe, even those that get high marks in good governance. But here we are talking about a pattern of behaviour that is widely accepted and expected in a society – or at least in large segments of its population. Two well-known and authoritative Latin Americans offer excellent insights on the matter. Ecuador's former president, Osvaldo Hurtado, explains the absence of solid norms and values of impartiality in his home country: "Personal merits are not recognized and rewarded due to the power and influence that personal relations have in a stratified and paternalistic society in which many decisions are based on the exchange of loyalty and favors ..." Further, Hurtado adds that "nepotism and favors for "buddies" are commonly present. The relationship between relatives and friends is so strong that the person who does not accept the request and does not place them in bureaucratic positions causes resentment among those affected, to whom it would never occur to think about whether the person was deserving of the position or not".

> *The State is impersonal; the Argentine can only conceive of personal relations. Therefore, to him, robbing public funds is not a crime. I am noting a fact; I am not justifying or excusing it...*
>
> – *Jorge Luis Borges*

What Hurtado says about Ecuador applies generally to the rest of Latin America. Renowned journalist and writer Carlos Alberto Montaner laments that "a large percentage of Latin Americans either nurture or tolerate relationships in which personal loyalty is rewarded and merit is substantially ignored. In Latin American culture, loyalty rarely extends beyond the circle of friends and family. Thus the public sector is profoundly mistrusted and the notion of the common good is very weak". Montaner further affirms that perceived power in Latin America resides in the ability to operate above the law.

One of the world's experts on political development and governance, Francis Fukuyama, echoes these observations: "In many Latin American societies, a narrow radius of trust produces a two-tier moral system, with good behaviour reserved for family and personal friends, and a decidedly lower standard of behaviour in the public sphere. This serves as a cultural foundation for corruption, which is often regarded as a legitimate way of looking after one's family... [In] much of Latin America, social capital resides largely in families and a rather narrow circle of personal friends. It is difficult for people to trust those beyond these narrow circles. Strangers fall into a different category than kin; a lower standard of moral behaviour applies when one becomes, for example, a public official. This provides cultural reinforcement for corruption: in such societies; one feels entitled to steal on behalf of one's family."

In empirical studies, social scientists demonstrate the cultural underpinnings of favouritism, not only in Latin America but also other countries and regions. In Nepal, an original survey contained a series of thirteen questions to test for acceptance across seven types of corruption ranging from petty bribery to favouritism and nepotism. The survey results showed 'substantial variation in attitudes towards different types of corrupt behaviour... Overall, there was greater disagreement among citizens over patterns of behaviour beyond the typical bribery scenario, and the informal constraints against these forms of corruption may be weaker as a result'. The study confirms a clash between values emphasizing impartiality and local social norms emphasizing favouritism.

Anthropological studies in Benin, Niger and Senegal reach similar conclusions to the Nepal study, demonstrating that the legitimacy of a corrupt practice is highly context-dependent. Corruption has 'two faces', as argued by Blundo and Olivier de Sardan: "The first is overtly illegal and broadly condemned. The second is legitimised by social practices, tolerated and sometimes unofficially encouraged... actors adopt 'situational morality' depending on the position of the actor and the circumstances they are operating within." The authors explore the difference between corrupt practices that have social legitimacy (such as showing favouritism in how public services are dispersed) and corrupt practices that are both formally prohibited and decried as illegitimate. In the first category, where corrupt practices are socially legitimized and honest acts that diverge from this engrained value are socially rejected, the public official is expected to exploit his or her position to benefit their family and friends. The latter category (acts that are not socially accepted) includes those that do not redistribute benefits or that involve stealing private resources, such as acts of extortion or acts that are excessively greedy. Interestingly, the boundary between these two categories is fluid. For instance, theft and misappropriation are viewed negatively and seen as morally unacceptable, but 'become more acceptable when the perpetrator is known and when the "victim" is abstract, such as a public body'. It follows that in societies with deeply embedded clientelistic practices, changes in structures and incentives will not reach very far.

In Armenia, a study examined the perceptions and attitudes of professional integrity of teachers in public schools, and showed how favouritism and nepotism are widely shared social norms. Many of the teachers admitted showing preferential treatment to the sons and daughters of their colleagues. In many cases, these students were either given higher grades or allowed to copy in exams. This type of favouritism is a strong expectation among the teacher's community, and any deviation from such expected behaviour brought accusations of a lack of friendship and weak professional loyalty.

In Mexico, studies show the social acceptance of favouritism towards relatives and friends, whether to provide a legitimate service or to break the law. The exchange of favours is a deeply ingrained social custom, which people generally do not consider to be corruption. As one study points out: 'This system of favouritism is supported by cultural values of loyalty, trust and friendship, and is socially accepted and legitimate. Most ordinary people, and many public officials, don't view these patterns of behaviour as illegal, immoral or corrupt… this is a cultural problem that cannot be solved through legal or administrative measures.'

Many societies face a stronger clash of values: personal relationships or loyalty prevail over impartiality and equity. The feeling of guilt towards the corrupt partner, such as a relative, friend or colleague, is stronger than that towards the victim third party, whether other people or the community at large. In societies where the separation between the public and private spheres is weak, and where sentiments of loyalty are strong among family members, circles of friends or ethnic groups, corrupt practices are free from any moral reprobation when the beneficiary belongs to the insider group. Unless values and norms of good governance are internalized and a culture of legality is strengthened, societies will lack effective controls and restraints of corruption.

Strong institutions in society rest on strong values and norms. Integrity in public life depends not only on the right institutional structures, but most importantly on supportive values and norms. The functioning of institutions depends on, and reflects, cultural values and attitudes. As one African observer put it: ‘Culture is the mother, institutions are the children.’ As Transparency International has fully acknowledged, ethics, norms and values are foundational to the integrity system of countries. According to such organization, the integrity system of a country may be compared with a Greek temple where the pillars represent the different public and private institutions in society with a role in promoting and protecting public integrity.

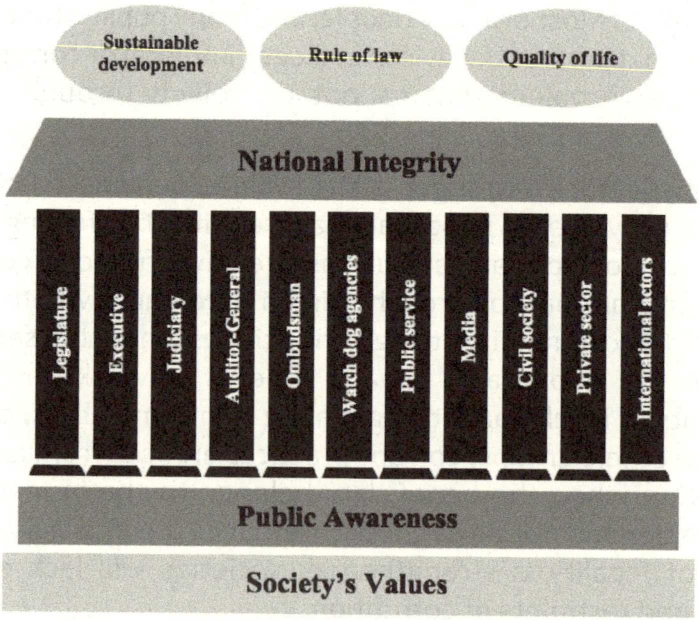

5. The Christian Faith and Church: A Platform for Building a Culture of Public Integrity

A sweeping reform of religion may be sufficient to bring cultural change.

– Lawrence Harrison

Corruption is not beyond culture; it is an intricate part of culture in many societies, springing in part from a lack of strong values and social norms around good governance. This problem is not just about inadequate laws or deficient institutions, or simply a question of individual greed and personal venality, but a deficit in the public morality of a community. In societies where a high level of social legitimization of corruption exists alongside low levels of compliance with the law, poor interpersonal trust and poor trust in public institutions, what is needed more than anything is a cultural revolution: a deep awakening that openly displays the destructive effects of the social norms that propagate corruption, along with a radical shift in mindset.

It would be a complete over-generalization to say that everyone in a society acts corruptly because it is the social expectation, and that not acting in such a way is illogical and foolish. There is no doubt that in many cases there is likely to be an element of pragmatic resignation, even survival, that leads a person to commit an act of corruption, even if they believe it is immoral and unacceptable. However, there are many other cases in which the corrupt act – whether favouritism or nepotism – is perceived as acceptable and not morally rejected. Be it a question of resignation and pragmatism or a legitimizing and accepting of this act, a profound cultural revolution is needed, starting with leaders in all areas of society.

Without values and social norms that sustain public integrity, institutions will not be effective in reducing corruption. In his widely acclaimed *Culture Matters*, co-author and former professor and researcher at Harvard University, the late Lawrence Harrison, affirms that it is necessary to strengthen cultural capital. We need to put a stronger emphasis on values and norms of public integrity at the personal and social levels. Without a cultural transformation, it will not be possible to achieve a sustainable and genuine improvement in governance.

The true empowerment of civil society comes through changing the rules of the game of governance. It is not only about strengthening demand for good governance, as if there were a sharp divide between citizens and public servants, where citizens should be empowered to demand the integrity of their leaders. It is not enough to create mechanisms of transparency and accountability if society does not trust, nor expects its public servants or other members of society to act with honesty and integrity. It is about a social transformation that transcends the traditional dichotomies of state-and-civil-society and goes beyond reforms of supply and demand. A cultural focus offers a cross-cutting conceptualization of the problem that connects agents and institutions of all sectors of society.

The questions remain: What do we do to change this situation? How can we strengthen and sustain social norms for good governance? Is it possible to develop a culture of public integrity?

Why the Christian Faith and Church?

The Christian faith has a strong presence and influence across the world. Christianity is a pre-eminent system of belief in almost every country in Latin America and Africa, and has a strong historical presence in the United States and Europe. In Latin America, people professing the Christian faith exceed 90% of the respective populations in almost all countries. The majority of those who declare to be Christians are from the Catholic tradition, though Protestant congregations have been growing substantially in recent decades. Although not everyone who identifies as Christian is committed to their faith, the percentages of those who consider Christianity to be important and who are active members of their local congregation are quite significant.

The Christian church, through its leaders, institutions and believers, generally has a potential role in the social transformation needed in Latin America and other regions to build up public integrity. However, their possible contribution to this transformation has not captured attention in the global anti-corruption agenda. The church, and religious faith in general, is a marginal theme in academic studies and programmes about corruption. Religion and religious actors are hardly mentioned in the work and deliberations of experts when referring to the fight against corruption, or even in discussions about the role of civil society in particular. Religious leaders continue to have a limited role in global movements about integrity and governance. In fact, 'the role of religious organizations is reduced to, at best, a hidden place as one of the many interest groups that might make up an active civil society', and could play a more pivotal role to positively influence integrity and value systems. In the global anti-corruption agenda that has remained predominantly institutional and technocratic, the church has remained sequestered as a sub-sector of civil society, without any consideration about how religious faith can motivate cultural change. The role of the church remains instrumental rather than intrinsic; religious organizations are recognized in their humanitarian role and social mission to protect the sick, orphans and marginalized, but rarely is their role considered in the formation of values and attitudes.

In considering the role of the church in more detail, the following key questions naturally emerge:

- Why should the church be considered in the fight against corruption? What factors would motivate us to consider that it should play a central role?
- What are the challenges that the church faces in the fight against corruption? What factors prevent or inhibit its acting as an agent of cultural change?
- What are the opportunities that the church has in the fight against corruption? What can or should it do?

This chapter deals with the first question and the next chapter considers the second and third questions.

While there are surely other factors, we highlight three that motivate us to consider the central role that the church should play in the fight against corruption. First, the Christian faith has a global reach and influence. Secondly, justice and good governance are part of the Christian identity and integral mission of the church. Finally, one cannot overlook the example and legacy of historic reforms that have brought about significant social changes which were motivated by the Christian faith through its leaders and believers. A few thoughts on each factor follow.

Factor 1: Christianity has Global Influence

To start with, religion is an important, if not the most important, source of internalized values and norms in a large number of societies. The presence and importance of religion in a person's life is growing in the majority of the world. Religion continues as a vital force for the majority of the globe; in effect, religion 'is fundamental to people as they try to make sense of and give meaning to their lives, and because it is one of the primary sources of values and morality for the majority of the world's population'. Christianity is the world's largest religion and the predominant one in many regions and countries. As an example, the following two tables show the reach and significance of the Christian faith in Latin America:

	% Christian	% Catholic	% Protestant	% Other Christian	% Other Religion	% None
Argentina	87	71	15	1	6	6
Bolivia	95	77	16	2	1	3
Brazil	88	61	26	1	4	7
Chile	83	64	17	2	6	11
Colombia	93	79	13	1	1	5
Costa Rica	88	62	25	1	1	8
Dominican Republic	81	57	23	1	0	18
Ecuador	94	79	13	2	1	4
El Salvador	88	50	36	2	0	12
Guatemala	92	50	41	1	1	6
Honduras	88	46	41	1	2	9
Mexico	92	81	9	2	4	3
Nicaragua	91	50	40	1	2	6
Panama	91	70	19	2	2	6
Paraguay	97	89	7	1	1	1
Peru	95	76	17	2	1	3
Uruguay	60	42	15	3	16	24
Venezuela	91	73	17	1	3	6

Table 2: Religious Affiliation in Latin America

	Argentina	Brazil	Chile	Colombia	Mexico	Peru	Uruguay
% who go to religious services once a week or more, apart from weddings and funerals	20.0	49.9	23.5	48.3	46.2	39.7	12.3
% who are active members in a church or religious organization	17.0	49.5	23.1	49.1	37.6	21.1	12.6
"Do you think that churches are giving adequate answers to moral problems?" (% who responded 'Yes')*	35.2	60.6	46.9	66.2	55.1	54.2	39.2
"Do you think that churches are giving adequate answers to social problems facing society?" (% who responded 'Yes')*	34.2	45.1	42.9	66.0	46.3	49.7	29.2
"How important is God in your life?" (% who responded "Very important")	28.4	87.5	41.1	85.1	79.7	60.5	25.9
"How important is religion in your life?" (% who responded 'Very important')	24.1	51.5	23.8	58.9	58.4	49.9	20.3

* These questions come from World Values Survey Wave 5; the rest come from World Values Survey Wave 6.

Table 3: Religiosity in Latin America

Factor 2: Promoting Public Integrity and Justice are Part of the Integral Mission of the Church

Secondly, public integrity and justice are part of the Biblical mandate and part of the integral mission of the church. Corruption denies the good news of God, who is Justice. Corruption is injustice and these are themes that permeate the entirety of Scripture. A deep theological analysis of this subject exceeds the scope of this book, but some brief reflections are included below.

Gary Haugen, president of the Christian NGO, International Justice Mission, writes in his book *Good News about Injustice: A Witness of Courage in a Hurting World,* Scripture teaches four truths about justice:

- God loves justice and, conversely, hates injustice.
- God has compassion for those who suffer injustice – everywhere around the world, without distinction or favour.
- God judges and condemns those who perpetrate injustice.
- God seeks active rescue for the victims of injustice.

God has a passion for justice, as expressed by the prophet Jeremiah: 'Thus says the Lord: "Let not the wise man glory in his wisdom, Let not the mighty man glory in his might, Nor let the rich man glory in his riches; But let him who glories glory in this, That he understands and knows Me, That I am the Lord, exercising loving-kindness, judgement, and righteousness in the earth. For in these I delight."'

God has a holy hatred of injustice, as reflected in the Psalms: 'God is a just judge, And God is angry with the wicked every day... The Lord tests the righteous, But the wicked and the one who loves violence His soul hates. Upon the wicked He will rain coals; Fire and brimstone and a burning wind Shall be the portion of their cup. For the Lord is righteous, He loves righteousness; His countenance beholds the upright.' Injustice exists when power or authority is misused in a way that deprives others from what God has given them, like life, dignity and the fruits of their work.

God has compassion for those who suffer injustices, and teaches us throughout all of Scripture that he sees and hears the cry of the oppressed. God condemns those who commit injustice. God hates injustice just as he hates idolatry and responds to injustice with indignation. Finally, God desires that the oppressor – the guilty – be brought to justice.

Corruption is a perversion of justice and a violation of the love of God and neighbour. Scripture is very clear about corruption: bribes and the use of influence to gain unjust outcomes are unacceptable forms of behaviour and are inconsistent with the will of God:

- And you shall take no bribe, for a bribe blinds the discerning and perverts the words of the righteous. (Exodus 23:8, New King James Version)
- You shall not pervert justice; you shall not show partiality, nor take a bribe, for a bribe blinds the eyes of the wise and twists the words of the righteous. (Deuteronomy 16:19, New King James Version)

- A wicked man accepts a bribe behind the back to pervert the ways of justice. (Proverbs 17:23, New King James Version)
- For I know your manifold transgressions and your mighty sins: Afflicting the just and taking bribes; Diverting the poor from justice at the gate. (Amos 5:12, New King James Version)
- Surely oppression destroys a wise man's reason, and a bribe debases the heart. (Ecclesiastes 7:7, New King James Version)
- That they may successfully do evil with both hands – the prince asks for gifts, the judge seeks a bribe, and the great man utters his evil desire; so they scheme together. (Micah 7:3, New King James Version)

The Christian leader, Joel Edwards, enumerates various Biblical stories that demonstrate the rejection of corrupt behaviour. Among them, Ahab and his wife Jezabel's abuse of power, perpetrated through the manipulation of justice and false witnesses, to illegally acquire Naboth's vineyard, and the corresponding prophetic outcry by the prophet Elijah (1 Kings 21); Nehemiah's action to end the extortion of the people of Judah by its nobles and officials, and his ordering the restitution of illegally acquired goods (Nehemiah 5); Jesus' purification of the Temple, condemning the merchants' extortion (Mark 11:15-19); Jesus' command to pay taxes to the state (Mark 12:13-17); and the manipulation of justice, bribes and false testimony in the context of the crucifixion and resurrection of Jesus Christ.

Factor 3: Christianity has a History of Sparking Change

Thirdly, the Christian faith has inspired and motivated cultural and social transformation throughout history, including good governance. Key social justice reforms during the nineteenth century, like the abolition of slavery, prison reform, women's rights and legislation against child labour, have been motivated largely by the Christian faith. Sydney Ahlstrom, historian at the University of Yale, believes that it is impossible to understand the humanitarian movement of the nineteenth century United States without recognizing the collective conscience and social commitment of evangelical Christianity at the time.

Historians, political scientists, economists and academics from other disciplines have specifically recognized that the Protestant Reformation has had a significant impact on the promotion of good governance. Some argue that historical Protestantism, in contrast to hierarchical religious traditions, has exercised greater tolerance enabling individuals to dissent and to challenge authority. One cannot ignore the fact that Martin Luther's protest against corruption present in the Vatican and the sale of indulgences was a key factor in the origin of the Protestant movement. In societies where hierarchical religions predominate, complaints against politicians and public servants could be less frequent than in societies that are moulded by more individualistic or egalitarian religions like Protestantism. Others believe that Protestant societies emphasize individual responsibility and the need to be virtuous. This influences how people perceive their loyalties to family and curbs the tendency to nepotism. It is also believed that the separation of Church and State is more pronounced in the Protestant tradition, which has facilitated the development of a more autonomous, active and effective civil society in the monitoring and supervision of the State.

Francis Fukuyama, thinker and renowned political science author, writes about the importance of the religious factor in the promotion of good governance. He explains the contrasts between the cases of Germany, the United Kingdom and the United States on the one hand, and Greece and Italy on the other. He asks how it is that the first group has been more successful in developing a state that operates less on a basis of patronage and more on a basis of impartiality and respect for the law. Although Fukuyama admits there is no direct mechanism to ensure the production of an honest and modern government, he suggests that there are cultural factors, among others, that explain the different results of these groups of countries. There is a high level of morality associated with the social movements that produced more honest governments in Germany, the UK and the US. In each country's reform movements there have been leaders that were motivated by their personal faith, including Frederick William I of Prussia, the Puritans of England from before the English Civil War of the seventeenth century, and the progressive reformers in the United States from the end of the nineteenth century to the beginning of the twentieth.

6. The Christian Faith and the Church: Challenges and Opportunities in Promoting a Culture of Public Integrity

We now address the remaining two questions about the role of the church in fighting corruption:

- What are the challenges that the church faces in the fight against corruption? What factors prevent or inhibit its acting as an agent of cultural change?
- What are the opportunities that the church has in the fight against corruption? What can or should it do?

The Challenges

Although there are solid foundations for the church to play a protagonist role in the fight against corruption, the challenges found along the way are quite significant. One might expect a religious society to exhibit a higher level of public morality than a less religious one. Many assume that, in the countries where religion plays an essential role in daily living for the majority of the population, public figures would also derive their ethics from religion and be influenced away from committing acts of corruption. However, if we look at existing data, this assumption does not appear to coincide with reality. The evidence points to the fact that religion in general – Christianity included – has a somewhat limited impact on the attitudes and behaviour in regard to public morality as it relates to corruption.

Little Evidence of Success

Put simply, many Christian-majority societies are the same societies where corruption is endemic.

For example, let us consider the specific situation of the Christian church and corruption in Latin America, which has relevance for other countries and regions. First, one must note how a great number of these countries have correspondingly high percentages of Christians and high levels of corruption (see *Appendix 1: Selected Country Data*). Corruption is a serious problem in Latin American countries with Christian-majority populations, even in those where there is a significant and growing presence of Protestant and evangelical churches. If Protestantism did, in fact, have a historic impact towards good governance in Europe, the United States and Canada, it appears that the relationship between Protestantism and better governance is not automatic. Protestantism – particularly evangelical Protestantism – has grown exponentially since the beginning of the twentieth century, and particularly so in the most recent decades in Latin America. In 1900, evangelicals accounted for 700,000 people, or 1% of the population. In 2010, they numbered 91 million, accounting for 16.8% of the population. However, their impact on the reduction of corruption seems minimal and definitely lower than those countries with an older Protestant tradition.

It can be argued that religion is just one factor that exists among many other social and institutional factors that are deeply rooted and take a long time to change. Robert D. Woodberry, professor of political science at the National University of Singapore, says: "When people convert to a new religious tradition or leave religion altogether, they do not automatically change all their beliefs and assumptions; they do not automatically change their expectations and interpretations of others; they do not automatically change the institutions that govern society. These changes take time and the co-operation of others."

It could also be that churches and their leaders, including those of Protestant denominations, fail to promote the values and patterns of behaviour that foster good governance. There is a high level of religiosity, but very little internalization of the values and patterns of behaviour that encourage public morality. Today, the countries with less corruption, like those of northern Europe, are those with a historic Protestant tradition but which are now predominantly secular.

Two Pioneering Studies: Does Christian Faith Affect People's Attitudes and Patterns of Behaviour towards Corruption?

Two studies offer preliminary and significant data about the influence of the Christian faith and the church on the attitudes and behaviour of people. In the first study, Martin Allaby, British public health doctor and researcher, offers an empirical study about the attitudes of evangelicals when confronted with corruption. Allaby conducted studies in Peru, the Philippines, Kenya and Zambia. Each of these countries has an absolute majority of Christians and high levels of corruption. In each country, Allaby interviewed a group of key stakeholders about how the evangelical church contributes to the reduction of corruption in their country. Using a semi-structured interview method, the research covered three broad questions:

- To what extent do evangelicals in each country have a reputation for honest behaviour?
- Where corruption within the evangelical sector is perceived to be a problem, what do evangelical leaders see as the causes?
- To what extent do evangelical leaders in each country think that evangelicals are effective in opposing corruption, be it through the promotion of honest behaviour through evangelical preaching, reforming government by having evangelicals in the government, and in promoting civic oversight of government?

In each country, five different groups were interviewed: leaders of evangelical churches, denominations and umbrella bodies; evangelicals who held leadership positions as professionals, in business or in evangelical NGOs working in the area of social justice; representatives from secular NGOs working in the area of anti-corruption; senior staff in government agencies with the responsibility for controlling corruption, such as anti-corruption commissions and auditor general's offices; and representatives of major non-evangelical churches, particularly from the Catholic Church.

Allaby found that the reputations of the evangelical churches' level of honesty varied significantly between all four countries. When evangelicals were in the minority of a society, their reputation was generally positive while, on the contrary, when they represented the main religious group, their reputation was not. According to Allaby, this difference would appear to obey sociologists' distinction between the 'church' and a 'sect' where the latter is applied to groups of Christians who are the minority in society and who carry higher expectations for upright social conduct and in a state of greatest tension with the country's predominant culture.

Despite the perceived difference between evangelicals in the minority or majority, the study highlights that the differences are relative and that evangelicals, even when in the minority, participate in corrupt practices.

In the case of Latin America, Allaby's findings show that evangelical leaders in Peru agreed that there is no preaching or teaching about corruption in evangelical churches. On the other hand, they also affirmed that the evangelical community lacked any general awareness towards social activism or taking a prophetic role. The fight against corruption was not perceived to be part of the mission of the church. One interviewed leader in Peru stated: "The church is focused on saying, 'Corruption is wrong, let's be sure we're not corrupt', but not on saying, 'Let's fight the existing corruption.'" The church has not adopted a prophetic role in denouncing acts of corruption. The mobilization of evangelicals for a better government is not on its agenda. In this aspect of the social role of the church, evangelical leaders admitted that these deficiencies were a result of a dualistic theology, something which promotes the belief that Christians should deal only with spiritual, and not with political, concerns.

In the second study, which I led, Taylor University (Indiana, United States) and the University of Azuay (Cuenca, Ecuador) collaborated in realizing the first phase of an empirical study about the relationship between Christian faith and attitudes towards corruption. It was conducted in the city of Cuenca, Ecuador, and consisted of two parts: a quantitative survey and a qualitative semi-structured interview.

The initial results of the survey, although not yet conclusive, indicate that high levels of general religiosity do not have a significant impact on ethical reasoning. See *Appendix 2: Cuenca Survey* for further details and sample questions.

The qualitative interviews provided complementary results to the survey. Those interviewed agreed upon the severity of the problem of corruption and its rootedness in Cuenca's culture and society. In general, they described their society as permissive and indifferent to corruption. People do not report corruption out of fear of retaliation. According to the interviews, the most common form of corruption in Cuenca is favouritism, which shows up in different ways and in all sectors. The majority of those interviewed agreed that religion and the church should play an important role in reducing corruption; however, in general, the sentiment was that the church did not instil Biblical values of justice and public integrity.

The Opportunities

The argument of this book is not that the Christian church, its leaders and members, exhibit overall higher levels of integrity or public ethics compared with non-Christians, although there may be unexplored differences between the various groups and denominations of the church. Rather, the argument of this book is based on the belief that the church is not static nor without the possibility of internal change, but is instead dynamic with great potential for instigating cultural change. Now, this should not lead to a simplified line of reasoning – that religion could be a quick and easy solution to the problem of corruption. Assessing the potential that religion has to transform patterns of behaviour that are firmly rooted in a society should be done with caution.

As the church, we should be 'salt' and 'light' in our communities. This implies two lines of action, intricately related to each other, in which leaders and believers should fight against corruption. The first involves the church that is 'in the world' – connected to and invested in the social problems that affect its leaders and believers. The church should be a prophetic voice in society that demands justice and good governance from its government and other social actors. This is advocating public integrity. The second line of action involves the church that is 'not of this world' – that is to say, a church that demonstrates values and patterns of behaviour that are examples of good public morality and ethics. As Joel Edwards says: "Only a transformed church is likely to be an agent of transformation. Light shines out best when our windows are clean." This is demonstrating public integrity.

The Church that is 'In the World'

The prophet Micah offers an excellent model of how a religious leader exhorts politicians, religious people and society in general to demand public integrity. Micah clearly understood how devastating the effects of corruption were on society – especially for the poor – and how it violated the norms set out in the Old Testament. The prophet lived in an era where power and wealth were highly concentrated within a corrupt elite. The leaders of society abused their positions of authority to benefit personally – to the detriment of the community. They oppressed the less fortunate, exacerbating social inequality and undermining the foundations for a just and peaceful society. Corruption was not only a problem with the political and religious elite – fraudulent practices were present in the private sector as well. In fact, the prophet condemns wealth acquired through dishonest commercial practices, such as the defrauding of clients using unfair weights and measures.

In Micah's time, eighth century BC, Israel suffered from endemic corruption – and not only minor, but also grand corruption. There was a complete state capture by the powerful. Micah tells us: "That they may successfully do evil with both hands – the prince asks for gifts, the judge seeks a bribe, and the great man utters his evil desire; so they scheme together." Cheating, fraud and dishonesty were so rooted that it was impossible to trust anyone. Micah warns the Israelites: "Do not trust in a friend; do not put your confidence in a companion; guard the doors of your mouth from her who lies in your bosom." This level of social distrust is what we see and live with in many of our communities and societies today.

How did Micah react in the face of such an overwhelming reality? The prophet was not indifferent, but instead concerned himself with the moral decline of his nation. He was well-informed of the magnitude of corruption and its harmful effects on society, observing that corruption affected all sectors in society. Micah exposed corruption and made a public outcry about the injustice. He confronted the corrupt political and religious leaders. He understood that Israel could not prosper unless society changed its corrupt and oppressive practices.

The Micahs of Today

Today, there are Christian leaders and organizations that are fully exercising their prophetic voice to expose corruption – in some cases, at great personal risk. Two impressive cases include: the global 'Exposed' campaign by the Micah Network and the Association for a More Just Society in Honduras.

'Exposed' called Christians around the world to mobilize to demand that churches, businesses and governments adopt practical and political action to resist corruption. The campaign was launched in 2012 by a coalition of, among others, the Micah Challenge, the Bible Society (England & Wales), the American Bible Society, the Salvation Army and the World Evangelical Alliance. 'Exposed' represented a historic act by being the first time that Christian organizations and agencies unified to denounce corruption publicly.

The campaign culminated in a petition to the G20 meeting in Brisbane, Australia, in November 2014. The petition contained the signatures of approximately 150,000 people from 188 countries. At the same time, a letter was signed by 95 international Christian leaders who represented a community of more than one billion people. The petition and letter required the G20 leaders to implement reforms to the global financial system to combat tax evasion and money laundering.

The Association for a More Just Society in Honduras (AJS) is a Christian civil society organization founded in 1998. It currently serves as a national chapter for Transparency International. They identify themselves as a group of 'brave Christians dedicated to making Honduras' system of laws and government work properly to Do Justice for the poor and inspiring other Christians to Do Justice'. Their aim is to work with genuine resolve for a society where justice prevails – especially for the most vulnerable – through just legislation, its equitable application and through the participation of the church, society and the state.

AJS conducts research into corruption, reports acts of corruption and promotes reform through practical proposals and legal means. Their anti-corruption initiatives cover various sectors, including education and health. In the area of education, they conducted a study into corruption and its connection with the absenteeism of teachers and professors. Through this research and other reports from AJS, the government was successfully pressured to take corrective action. This resulted in a substantial reduction of absentee teachers and professors, and a significant improvement in the educational performance of the students. In the area of health, AJS researched and found overcharging for medicines as well as other corrupt acts committed by the government. This research catalyzed a complete reform of the system of procurement of medicine in Honduras, in collaboration with an independent entity and social audits.

Of course, the prophetic role of the church and its leaders is intimately related to, and affected by, their own credibility and integrity. This leads to the second, and crucial, line of action.

The Church that is 'Not of the World'

The church should be an active participant in demanding that there be more transparency and accountability of political leaders and public servants. However, as explored in previous chapters, the emphasis on social control has, until this point, centred on laws, institutions and formal processes rather than on any profound change of values and attitudes. These laws, institutions and processes of good governance only offer a framework – although a necessary one – that facilitates the implementation of behavioural change. However, if there is no deep change in the pre-eminent values and attitudes that legitimize and tolerate corruption, the formal institutional structures will not be effective and, in fact, could be the object of abuse or manipulation. We need transformation of cultural norms for institutional changes to be sustainable.

The evidence seems to suggest that the church in general is not forming or modelling the values of public integrity. As pointed out by the theologian Yahya Wijaya from Indonesia, the messages about social ethics are less explicit in churches. Although there is Biblical teaching against corruption, believers still participate in corrupt practices and are not always aware that these practices are inconsistent with the teaching of Scripture. Joel Edwards explains that the first task of the church in combating corruption is to become aware that God does not tolerate corruption, and that the subject is practically ignored in its theological understanding and teaching of the Bible.

The abuse of power and breach of public trust are not preaching, teaching or discipleship subjects in churches. Corruption as a cause of profound social injustice is not understood, nor seen as a priority. As recognized by various religious leaders and other experts, 'Faith-based organizations can be blind to the importance of good governance. People who identify themselves as religious make up at least three quarters of the world's population; as such, they also make up a large proportion of the people who give and take bribes. If anti-corruption was incorporated into the ethics of religion, this could have some impact on bribery; we might be able to build a global moral consensus not to accept bribery.'

The above applies not only to bribes, but also, and potentially more importantly depending on the local context, to other forms of corruption in which many cases enjoy major acceptance or social legitimacy. The tolerance, and even the admiration in some cases, of those who take advantage of public confidence for private gain are some of the many practices that undermine the public good.

Among the initiatives to reform the ethics within the church, it is worth mentioning the efforts that have been undertaken in the Christian church in India. In his book, *Corruption-Free Churches are Possible,* Swiss author and professor, Christoph Stückelberger highlights a series of initiatives by Christian leaders and institutions in India. Various religious leaders admit that the Christian church is just as corrupt as society in general. For example, Stückelberger mentions cases of corruption of church leaders buying votes in the election of a bishop, paying bribes to gain positions in educational and church institutions, the misappropriation of funds and church properties, the payment of bribes in the construction of property, and retaliation against those who report acts of corruption. Faced with this tragic and sad reality, many religious leaders and organizations in India have united to promote a deep reform of governance in the church.

Among the many efforts realized in India is one that deserves mention: Operation Nehemiah is a movement to strengthen the transparency, accountability and financial integrity of the Christian church of India. The movement was started and is led by a group of businesspeople and professionals that have a desire to serve other Christian leaders and institutions in India. Operation Nehemiah seeks to facilitate church leaders' introspection and rejuvenation of attitudes and practices of governance by mobilizing prayer groups and forming small groups that support and follow up with leaders.

If the Christian faith does not translate into ethical behaviour that is exemplary and alternative to the world, and the church does not hold a prophetic role in the world, we as church leaders and believers should ask ourselves why this situation exists. It is essential for church leaders and believers to critically evaluate the condition of our values, attitudes and practices of governance and public integrity, and the extent to which we are captive to social norms of corruption. Once we are aware that our attitudes and behaviour do not coincide with the Biblical mandate or with our identity as Christians, only then will reformation be possible.

As believers, we have an opportunity and responsibility to wake up to the devastating consequences of this social sin and challenge ourselves towards radical change.

Appendix 1. Selected Country Data

This Appendix compiles relevant information about Christianity, corruption and anti-corruption work taking place across the world. The 64 countries appearing in this list are those which fit two criteria: 1) CPI 2017 score 50 or less and 2) Christian population 50% or more, organized by region, then sorted by CPI score. This Appendix does not cover all the relevant information about corruption, but is intended to represent an introductory amount of data that is broadly applicable to the globe. Many other corruption measures, Christian data and organizations doing anti-corruption exist and are just as relevant to the issue.

	CPI 2017	Christianity (% of pop)	World Bank Projects 1991-2017	USAID Projects 2007-2013
Africa	**CPI**	**Christian**	**WB**	**USAID**
South Sudan	12	61%	2	
Equatorial Guinea	17	88%	2	
Angola	19	93%		1
Democratic Republic of Congo	21	95%	2	2
Congo	21	89%	3	
Burundi	22	93%	1	2
Zimbabwe	22	82%		
Central African Republic	23	73%	2	
Madagascar	24	58%	5	1
Cameroon	25	59%		
Mozambique	25	53%	5	1
Uganda	26	84%	5	2
Kenya	28	81%	2	4
Malawi	31	80%	2	1
Gabon	32	85%	1	
Ethiopia	35	59%	2	1
Tanzania	36	55%	6	1
Zambia	37	85%	3	3
Swaziland	39	88%		
Ghana	40	64%	8	2
Lesotho	42	92%	1	
South Africa	43	82%		
Sao Tome & Principe	46	96%		

Asia	CPI	Christian	WB	USAID
Russia	29	82%	3	5
Philippines	34	91%	6	12
East Timor	38	88%	1	6
Europe	**CPI**	**Christian**	**WB**	**USAID**
Ukraine	30	86%	3	9
Moldova	31	97%	3	7
Armenia	35	94%	1	4
Macedonia	35	64%	4	7
Serbia	41	89%	2	5
Bulgaria	43	83%	1	1
Belarus	44	77%		
Hungary	45	87%		
Montenegro	46	78%	1	3
Romania	48	99%		
Greece	48	90%		
Croatia	49	94%	1	
Slovakia	50	85%		
Italy	50	77%		

Latin America and the Caribbean	CPI	Christian	WB	USAID
Venezuela	18	93%		
Haiti	22	94%	5	1
Nicaragua	26	95%	2	5
Guatemala	28	97%	7	5
Mexico	29	96%	1	2
Honduras	29	96%	2	3
Paraguay	29	95%	3	4
Dominican Republic	29	95%	2	7
Ecuador	32	95%	1	3
El Salvador	33	96%	2	4
Bolivia	33	93%	3	2
Peru	37	96%	2	5
Colombia	37	95%	1	4
Brazil	37	91%		
Panama	37	90%		1
Argentina	39	90%	4	
Trinidad & Tobago	41	63%	1	
Suriname	41	51%		
Guyana	38	54%		2
Jamaica	44	85%		1
Cuba	47	61%		

Oceania	CPI	Christian	WB	USAID
Papua New Guinea	29	95%		
Solomon Islands	39	95%		
Vanuatu	43	93%		

CPI: The Corruption Perceptions Index is a global measure of the perceived levels of corruption in the public sector. It ranks countries and territories based on how corrupt their public sector is perceived to be. A country or territory's score indicates the perceived level of corruption in the public sector on a scale of 0 to 100, where 0 means that a country is perceived as highly corrupt and 100 means it is perceived as having the highest level of public integrity. In the 2017 CPI, more than two-thirds of countries scored below 50, with an average score of 43. A country's rank indicates its position relative to the other countries and territories included in the index. The 2017 CPI includes 180 countries and territories.

Christianity (% of population): The percentage of people self-identifying as Christian is reported. Data is provided by the World Christian Database, with much of their data on Christianity coming from national censuses of 2015.

World Bank Projects 1991–2017: The World Bank designs and implements anti-corruption programmes. The projects reported here were found by searching 'corruption' in the World Bank Projects database and filtering out the 'Other accountability/anti-corruption' theme, resulting in 275 results as of 21st May 2018.

USAID Projects 2007–13: USAID's Anticorruption Projects Database includes information about USAID projects with anti-corruption interventions implemented worldwide between 2007 and 2013. After reviewing approximately 2,000 projects, about 300 were selected to be part of the database if they were distinctive interventions that targeted reducing corruption or promoting government integrity, accountability and transparency that ultimately resulted in reducing opportunities for corruption, and if there was sufficient information available about the project.

Appendix 2. Cuenca Survey

This project in the city of Cuenca, Ecuador, aimed to study the influence of Christian faith on peoples' perceptions, attitudes and behaviour related to public integrity, ultimately aspiring to guide the church towards a more effective response in promoting public integrity and reducing corruption. The research included surveys and interviews administered to Christians (Catholics and Protestant/evangelicals) and non-Christians. It followed a mixed-methods design, integrating quantitative surveys and qualitative interviews.

The quantitative data was collected through a survey from participants from Cuenca, Ecuador. The survey included demographic information, the Intrinsic Religious Motivation Scale and 17 hypothetical situations that reflected unique modes of ethical reasoning (Situationalist, Preconventionalist/Fear, Generalist, Antinomianist and Absolutist). Other questions about corruption in Ecuador were included for a more holistic understanding of the issue.

Asking participants about how they would respond in a hypothetical situation was a unique way in which this study sought to better understand the nuances of how people approach the complex issue of corruption. The hypothetical situations covered a wide variety of forms of corruption. Each hypothetical situation was presented alongside five different responses, representing each of the five modes of ethical reasoning. The participant was asked to assess their level of agreement for each of the five ways of responding, allowing the researchers to better understand how much of that mode of ethical reasoning the person identified with. Several hypothetical situations are included here as a sample of this approach.

Sample Questions

Please mark your level of agreement with the statements below by circling the response that best represents your opinion at this time, based on the scale below.

> **1–Definitely Would, 2–Very Good Chance,**
> **3–Some Chance, 4–Very Little Chance, 5–No Chance**

Imagine you are a public official at the Cuenca municipality and a vacancy opens in your department for a junior assistant position. The son of your best friend is looking for a job. You tell him to apply to the job. Several applicants apply to the job and some are more qualified than him. To what extent do you agree with the following statements?

- I would give the job to the son of my best friend because it might damage my relationship with my best friend.
- I would give the job to the son of my best friend because is a rather widespread practice to favour relatives and friends.

- I would give the job to the son of my best friend because there is little chance of getting caught and/or sanctioned for improper hiring processes.
- I would give the job to the best qualified person.

Imagine you are a department director at the Cuenca city government. For this fiscal year, the department budget has allocated resources for remodelling and refurbishing your department offices. Your sister owns and operates a company that sells office furniture. There are many other furniture stores in the city which can provide office furniture. There is little chance that anyone will monitor in detail the expenses made or become aware of your sister's connection with the furniture company. To what extent do you agree with the following statements?

- I would purchase the furniture from my sister; after all, one needs to help family.
- I would not purchase the furniture from my sister's company because of the conflict of interests.
- I would decide in favour of my sister's company; after all, you can only trust the quality of the furniture that comes from family or friends.
- I would decide in favour of my sister's company because no one would question the decision.

You are an expert on leadership and management matters. You have been hired by the municipality of Cuenca to organize a training programme on management issues for public officials. The training programme will last two days and take place outside the city in a summer resort location. Your contract with the City of Cuenca includes a travel fund (subject to a maximum) to cover necessary travel expenses. After dinner on one of the nights, you decide to go shopping and buy a few books for personal use. You have enough money in the travel fund to cover the expense of the books. To what extent do you agree with the following statements?

- I would choose to buy the books using the travel fund because it would make me better at my profession.
- I would not use the travel money to purchase the books because it would be a misuse of funds.
- I would choose to buy the books using the travel fund because it is a small amount of money and no one would notice.
- I would choose to buy the books using the travel fund because this is a widespread practice.

Imagine there are upcoming elections for mayor in Cuenca. Three candidates are running for office: the incumbent, a former mayor and a new politician. You are not affiliated with any political party. Representatives of each of the candidates have been visiting your neighbourhood to advocate for their candidate. You become aware that representatives of two of the candidates (the incumbent and the former mayor) have already been making gifts to voters to get their support. To what extent do you agree with the following statements?

- I would denounce these acts of corruption to the proper authorities.

- I would seek to secure a gift from the candidate I wished to vote for; after all, this is the way politics work and it is not fair that only others get gifts.
- I would vote for whichever candidate gave me the better gift.
- I would only support a candidate that did not give gifts to voters.

Imagine you are the owner of a restaurant in Cuenca. The Cuenca government inspector came today to inspect the safety and health conditions of the restaurant. He found defects for which I would need to pay a mandatory fine. To what extent do you agree with the following statements?

- I would offer a bribe to avoid paying the fine; after all, this is what the great majority of people do.
- I would pay the fine because the amount is not very significant.
- I would pay the fine because that is what the great majority of people do.
- I would contact my friend who is influential in the government to take care of the matter and avoid paying the fine.

Appendix 3. The Faith and Public Integrity Network

The Faith and Public Integrity Network (FPIN) is a learning community of Christian organizations striving to counter corruption in their local communities. FPIN provides a platform for member organizations to provide professional and personal support to other FPIN members, online and in person. Anti-corruption work is not easy – every organization doing this work benefits from being part of a supportive community of co-workers. The member site is kept private to maintain a level of confidentiality, privacy and connection among FPIN members.

FPIN creates broadly applicable country profiles, case profiles and other anti-corruption resources, as part of its commitment to provide useful and applicable resources that are relevant to the intersection of the Christian faith and public integrity. Country profiles uniquely combine and consolidate a country's data on religion, corruption and political liberties. Although FPIN does not currently generate this information, it does the work of curating relevant data from many other rigorous academic sources, including the Corruption Perceptions Index (by Transparency International), the Global Corruption Barometer (by Transparency International), World

Governance Indicators (by the World Bank), the Rule of Law Index (by the World Justice Project), the World Values Survey and the World Christian Database.

FPIN is supported by the Oxford Centre for Mission Studies (*www.ocms.ac.uk*), Faith in Government (*www.faithingovernment.org.uk*) and Fides (*http://fides-intl.org*).

Find the Faith and Public Integrity Network online at: *https://fpinetwork.wordpress.com* and *http://www.ocms.ac.uk/fpin*.

End Notes

Introduction

Micah 3:9-11 (MSG); 6:10-11 (MSG); 7:2, 3, 5 (ERV).

David Cameron, "Against Corruption: a collection of essays," London: Prime Minister's Office, 12 May 2016, accessed 21 May 2018, https://www.gov.uk/government/publications/against-corruption-a-collection-of-essays/against-corruption-a-collection-of-essays.

Proverbs 20:10 (NKJV).

Chapter 1

Genesis 6:11-12 (NKJV).

Eric Uslaner, Corruption, Inequality, and the Rule of Law: The Bulging Pocket Makes the Easy Life (New York: Cambridge University Press, 2010), 6.

"What is Corruption?" Transparency International, 2016, accessed 21 May 2018, http://www.transparency.org/what-is-corruption/.

"2017 FCPA Year-End Update," BakerHostetler, 2018, accessed 21 May 2018, https://www.bakerlaw.com/webfiles/Litigation/2018/Alerts/03-08-18-FCPA-2017-Year-end-Update.pdf; Yamil Santoro, "El kirchnerismo contra la ética pública," infobae opinión, 10 February 2016, accessed 21 May 2018, https://opinion.infobae.com/yamil-santoro/2016/02/10/el-kirchnerismo-contra-la-etica-publica/index.html; "Anti-Corruption: Public Health Reform," Association for a More Just Society, 2018, accessed 21 May 2018, https://www.ajs-us.org/what-we-do/anti-corruption.; "United States Seeks to Recover More Than $1 Billion Obtained from Corruption Involving Malaysian Sovereign Wealth Fund," Justice News: Department of Justice Office of Public Affairs, Press Release 16-839, 20 July 2016, accessed 21 May 2018, https://www.justice.gov/opa/pr/united-states-seeks-recover-more-1-billion-obtained-corruption-involving-malaysian-sovereign.; Scott Neuman, "Malaysian Police Seize Cash, Jewels, Designer Bags From Ousted Premier's Residence," the two-way: Breaking News from NPR, 18 May 2018, accessed 21 May 2018, https://www.npr.org/sections/thetwo-way/2018/05/18/612233783/malaysian-police-seize-cash-jewels-designer-bags-from-ousted-premiers-residence.

Transparency International, "Corruption Perceptions Index 2017," 21 February 2018, accessed 21 May 2018, https://www.transparency.org/research/cpi.

Chapter 2

The Secretary-General, "Statement On The Adoption By The General Assembly Of The United Nations Convention Against Corruption," New York, 31 October 2003, accessed 21 May 2018 at https://www.unodc.org/unodc/en/treaties/CAC/background/secretary-general-speech.html.

Daniel Kaufmann, "Myths and Realities of Governance and Corruption," Global Competitiveness Report 2005-2006, World Economic Forum, 2005, accessed 21 May 2018 at http://siteresources.worldbank.org/INTWBIGOVANTCOR/Resources/2-1_Governance_and_Corruption_Kaufmann.pdf.; "Global Financial Integrity 'Illicit Financial Flows from Developing Countries over the Decade Ending 2009,'" 2011, pg. i, accessed 21 May 2018, http://www.gfintegrity.org/storage/gfip/documents/reports/IFFDec2011/illicit_financial_flows_from_developing_countries_over_the_decade_ending_2009.pdf.

OECD, "Development aid rises again in 2016 but flows to poorest countries dip," 2017, accessed May 2018 at http://www.oecd.org/dac/development-aid-rises-again-in-2016-but-flows-to-poorest-countries-dip.htm

"Africa loses $148b to corruption annually," Vanguard, 25 January 2018, accessed May 2018, https://www.vanguardngr.com/2018/01/africa-loses-148b-corruption-annually/.

GTZ, "Mainstreaming Anti-Corruption," GTZ, Eschborn, 2004, 5.

"True Stories: Seeds of Change," Transparency International, 2018, accessed 21 May 2018, https://www.transparency.org/news/story/seeds_of_change.

Renato Raffaele Cardinal Martino and Giampaolo Crepaldi, Note of the Pontifical Council for Justice and Peace: "The Fight against Corruption," Vatican City, 21 September 2006, sec. 4 and 5, Feast of Saint Matthew, Apostle and Evangelist, accessed 21 May 2018, http://www.vatican.va/roman_curia/pontifical_councils/justpeace/documents/rc_pc_justpeace_doc_20060921_lotta-corruzione_en.html.

"EXPOSED - shining a light on corruption," Micah Challenge, 08 December 2011, accessed 21 May 2018, http://www.micahnetwork.org/news/exposed-shining-light-corruption.; "Anti-Corruption Campaign EXPOSED Launches on Thursday, Aiming at Mobilizing 100 Million Christians," World Evangelical Alliance, 10 October 2012, accessed 21 May 2018, http://worldea.org/news/4099/anti-corruption-campaign-exposed-launches-in-london-on-thursday-aiming-at-mobilizing-100-million-christians-by-october-2013.

Muir, David, Christine Romo, Xorje Olivares, "Haiti Six Months Later: Where Do Things Stand?" ABC News, 8 July 2010, accessed May 2018, https://abcnews.go.com/WN/haiti-earthquake-months-things-stand/story?id=11120059

Augusto Lopez Claros, "Removing Impediments to Sustainable Economic Development: The Case of Corruption," (Working Paper No. 6704, World Bank, 2013), 18-19.

Omar Azfar and Tugrul Gurgur, "Does Corruption Affect Health and Education Outcomes in the Philippines?" College Park: Institutional Reform and Informal Sector, 2008, accessed 21 May 2018, https://pdfs.semanticscholar.org/5a19/691b8ac651e7e39e7460509aa97db65c3f4a.pdf.

Ottar Maestad and Aziza Mwisongo, "Informal payments and the quality of health care: Mechanisms revealed by Tanzanian health workers," Health Policy 99 (2011): 107–115, accessed 21 May 2018, https://doi.org/10.1016/j.healthpol.2010.07.011.

Mohamed Dridi, "Corruption and Education: Empirical Evidence," International Journal of Economics and Financial Issues Mersin 4.3 (2014): 476-493, accessed 21 May 2018, http://www.econjournals.com/index.php/ijefi/article/view/781/pdf.

Transparency International, "Corruption Perceptions Index 2017." 21 February 2018, accessed 21 May 2018, https://www.transparency.org/research/cpi.

Matthieu Hanf, Astrid Van-Melle, Florence Fraisse, Amaury Roger, Bernard Carme, Mathieu Nacher, "Corruption Kills: Estimating the Global Impact of Corruption on Children Deaths," PLOS ONE 6.11 (2011): e26990, accessed 21 May 2018, https://doi.org/10.1371/journal.pone.0026990.

World Health organization, "By category > Mortality and global health estimates > Child mortality > Causes of child death > Number of deaths by cause > Number of deaths by region > World," Global Health Observatory data repository, accessed 21 May 2018, http://apps.who.int/gho/data/node.main.ChildMortREG1002015?lang=en.

World Bank, "Anti-corruption," (World Bank Brief, 2016), accessed 21 May 2018, http://www.worldbank.org/en/topic/governance/brief/anti-corruption.

TearFund, "Bribery Act: All parties rally behind landmark new law to fight corruption," Press Release, 9 April 2010, accessed 21 May 2018, https://www.globalwitness.org/archive/campaigners-applaud-passing-landmark-uk-bribery-bill/.

Transparency International, "Report on the Transparency International Global Corruption Barometer 2007," (Transparency International Report, Berlin, 2007), 2, accessed 21 May 2018, http://files.transparency.org/content/download/1980/12932/file/2007_GCB_EN.pdf.

"WCC calls churches to speak against corruption," World Council of Churches, 20 August 2013, accessed 21 May 2018, https://www.oikoumene.org/en/press-centre/news/wcc-calls-churches-to-speak-against-corruption.

"Evangelicals Shine a Light on Corruption at the G20 Summit in Brisbane," World Evangelical Alliance, Press Release, 14 November 2014, accessed 21 May 2018, http://www.worldea.org/news/4494/evangelicals-shine-a-light-on-corruption-at-the-g20-summit-in-brisbane.

Renato Raffaele Cardinal Martino and Giampaolo Crepaldi, Note of the Pontifical Council for Justice and Peace: "The Fight against Corruption," Vatican City, 21 September 2006, Feast of Saint Matthew, Apostle and Evangelist, accessed 21 May 2018, http://www.vatican.va/roman_curia/pontifical_councils/justpeace/documents/rc_pc_justpeace_doc_20060921_lotta-corruzione_en.html.

Chapter 3

Fukuyama, Francis. Political Order and Political Decay: From the Industrial Revolution to the Globalization of Democracy (New York: Macmillan, 2014) 162.

World Bank, "Helping Countries Combat Corruption: The Role of the World Bank," September 1997, accessed 21 May 2018, http://www1.worldbank.org/publicsector/anticorrupt/corruptn/corrptn.pdf. World Bank, "Helping Countries Combat Corruption: The Role of the World Bank," September 1997, accessed 21 May 2018, http://www1.worldbank.org/publicsector/anticorrupt/corruptn/corrptn.pdf.

World Bank, "Mainstreaming Anticorruption Activities in World Bank Assistance: A Review of Progress since 1997," World Bank, Washington, D.C., 2004, 27.; World Bank, "Helping Countries Combat Corruption: The Role of the World Bank," Poverty Reduction and Economic Management, Washington, D.C., September 1997, 21, accessed 21 May 2018, http://www1.worldbank.org/publicsector/anticorrupt/corruptn/corrptn.pdf.

Odd-Helge Fjeldstad and Jan Isaksen, "Anti-Corruption Reforms: Challenges, Effects and Limits of World Bank Support. Background Paper to Public Sector Reform: What Works and Why?," IEG

Evaluation of World Bank Support, World Bank, Washington, D.C., 2008, 6, 7, 92.

Ivar Kolstad, Verena Fritz, and Tam O'Neil, "Working Paper 3: Corruption, Anti-Corruption Efforts and Aid: Do Donors Have the Right Approach?," Research project (RP-05-GG) of the Advisory Board for Irish Aid, London, 2008, 43, accessed 21 May 2018, https://www.odi.org/sites/odi.org.uk/files/odi-assets/publications-opinion-files/2267.pdf.

David de Ferranti, Anthony J. Ody and Graeme Ramshaw, How to Improve Governance: A New Framework for Analysis and Action (Brookings Institution Press, 2009), 46-47.

Anna Persson, Bo Rothstein, and Jan Teorell, "Why Anticorruption Reforms Fail: Systemic Corruption as a Collective Action Problem," Governance Vol. 26.3 (2013): 449-471, 453.

World Bank, "World Bank Country-Level Engagement on Governance and Anticorruption: An Evaluation of the 2007 Strategy and Implementation Plan," Independent Evaluation Group Report, World Bank, 2011, 1, 41, 89, accessed 21 May 2018,
https://ieg.worldbankgroup.org/Data/Evaluation/files/gac_eval.pdf.

ITAD and LDP, "Joint Evaluation of Support to Anti-Corruption Efforts: 2002 – 2009," Norad Evaluation Report, Norwegian Agency for Development Cooperation, Oslo, 2011, 69, accessed 21 May 2018, https://www.norad.no/globalassets/import-2162015-80434-am/www.norad.no-ny/filarkiv/vedlegg-til-publikasjoner/joint-evaluation-of-support-to-anti-corruption-efforts-2002-2009.pdf.

Inter-American Development Bank, "Proposal for the Action Plan to Support the Countries in Their Efforts to Fight Corruption and Foster Transparency," PAACT, GN-2540, November 2009, 3, accessed 21 May 2018, http://idbdocs.iadb.org/wsdocs/getdocument.aspx?docnum=35008954.; World Bank, "Mainstreaming Anticorruption Activities in World Bank Assistance: A Review of Progress since 1997," World Bank, Washington, D.C., 2004.; Sarah Bracking, ed., Corruption and Development: The Anti-Corruption Campaigns (Basingstoke: Palgrave Macmillan, 2007).; Ed Brown and Jonathan Cloke, "Neoliberal Reform, Governance and Corruption in the South: Assessing the International Anti-Corruption Crusade," Antipode Vol. 36.2 (2004): 272–294, doi:10.1111/j.1467-8330.2004.00406.x.; Luís de Sousa, "Anti-Corruption Agencies: Between Empowerment and Irrelevance," Crime, Law and Social Change Vol. 53.1 (2011): 5–22, doi:10.1007/s10611-009-9211-3.; Alan Doig, David Watt, and Robert Williams, "Why Do Developing Country Anti-Corruption Commissions Fail to Deal with Corruption? Understanding the Three Dilemmas of Organizational Development, Performance Expectation, and Donor and Government Cycle," Public Administration and Development Vol. 27.3 (2007): 251– 259, doi:10.1002/pad.452.; Johnston, Michael, Syndromes of Corruption: Wealth, Power, and Democracy (New York: Cambridge University Press, 2005).; Timothy Lindsey and Howard W. Dick, ed., Corruption in Asia: Rethinking the Governance Paradigm (Leichhardt: The Federation Press, 2002).; Anna Persson, Bo Rothstein, and Jan Teorell, "The Failure of Anti-Corruption Policies: A Theoretical Mischaracterization of the Problem," University of Gothenberg QoG Working Paper Series 19, 2010, accessed 21 May 2018,
http://www.qog.pol.gu.se/digitalAssets/1350/1350163_2010_19_persson_rothstein_teorell.pdf.; Morris Szeftel, "Misunderstanding African Politics: Corruption and the Governance Agenda," Review of African Political Economy Vol. 25.76 (1998): 221-240, doi:10.1080/03056249808704311.; Jakob Svensson, "Eight Questions about Corruption," Journal of Economic Perspectives Vol. 19.3 (2005): 19-42, accessed 21 May 2018, http://kie.vse.cz/wp-content/uploads/Svensson-2005.pdf.; Heather Marquette, "'Finding God' or 'Moral Disengagement' in the Fight against Corruption in Developing Countries? Evidence from India and Nigeria," Public Administration and Development Vol. 32.1 (2012): 11-26, doi: 10.1002/pad.1605.

Recent empirical studies demonstrate that the anti-corruption reforms lack a solid empirical basis. They conclude that very few institutional reforms show positive, though inconclusive, results. Benjamin A. Olken, Rohini Pande, Iqbal Dhaliwal, Raluca Dragusanu, and Cristobal Marshall, "Governance Review Paper," Governance Initiative Review Paper, J-PAL Governance Initiative Abdul Latif Jameel Poverty Action Lab, May 2011, 12, accessed 21 May 2018, https://www.povertyactionlab.org/sites/default/files/documents/J-PAL_GI-ReviewPaper_vMay-2011.pdf.; Rema Hanna, Sarah Bishop, Sara Nadel, Gabe Scheffler, and Katherine Durlacher, "The Effectiveness of Anti-Corruption Policy: What Has Worked, What Hasn't, and What We Don't Know: A Systematic Review," EPPI-Centre Report No. 1909, 2011.;.; Jesper Johnsøn, "Theories of Change in Anti-Corruption Work: A Tool for Programme Design and Evaluation," U4 Issue no. 6 (2012), 24-25, accessed 21 May 2018, http://issuu.com/cmi-norway/docs/u4issue-2012-06-theories-of-change/1?e=0.

Eric M. Uslaner, "Corruption and Inequality" (UNUWIDER Research Paper No. 2006/34, United Nations University, 2006), 32.

Gaventa, John, y Rosemary McGee. "The Impact of Transparency and Accountability Initiatives". Development Policy Review Vol. 31.s1 (2013), 6, doi:10.1111/dpr.12017.

Fjeldstad, "Anti-Corruption Reforms," 7, 92, 17.

Jesper Johnsøn, "Theories of Change in Anti-Corruption Work: A Tool for Programme Design and Evaluation," U4 Issue no. 6 (2012), 12, accessed 21 May 2018, http://issuu.com/cmi-norway/docs/u4issue-2012-06-theories-of-change/1?e=05, 39; Gaventa, "The Impact of Transparency and Accountability Initiatives," 12.

Chapter 4

Lawrence E. Harrison and Samuel P. Huntington, ed., Culture Matters: How Values Shape Human Progress (New York: Basic Books, 2000), xv.

Francesca Recanatini, "Voices of the Misgoverned and Misruled: An Empirical Diagnostic Study on Governance, Rule of Law and Corruption for Peru" (World Bank Institute, Washington, D.C., 2001), 47, accessed 21 May 2018, http://siteresources.worldbank.org/INTANTICORRUPTION/Resources/383901-1317672198081/peru_voicesreport.pdf.

Fisman, "Cultures of Corruption."

World Bank, "Mainstreaming Anticorruption Activities in World Bank Assistance: A Review of Progress since 1997," World Bank, Washington, D.C., 2004, 37, 40.

Jorge Luis Borges, "Nuestro pobre individualismo," in Otras Inquisiciones (Buenos Aires: Emecé. 1996), 59-60.

Carlos Alberto Montaner, "Culture and the Behavior of Elites in Latin America" in Culture Matters: How Values Shape Human Progress, ed. Lawrence E. Harrison y Samuel P. Huntington (New York: Basic Books, 2000): 58-59. Ibid, 58.

Francis Fukuyama, "Social Capital and Civil Society," (Prepared for delivery at the IMF Conference on Second Generation Reforms, Washington, D.C., 1 October 1999), 8, accessed 21 May 2018, http://www.imf.org/external/pubs/ft/seminar/1999/reforms/fukuyama.htm.

Rory Truex, "Corruption, Attitudes, and Education: Survey Evidence from Nepal," World Development Vol. 39.7 (2011): 1133-1142, doi:10.1016/j.worlddev.2010.11.003.

Giorgio Blundo and Jean-Pierre Olivier de Sardan, Everyday Corruption and the State: Citizens & Pub-

lic Officials in Africa (London/New York: Zed Books, 2006).
Kolstad, "Corruption, Anti-Corruption Efforts and Aid," 27.; Francis Fukuyama, "Social Capital and Civil Society," 67.
Meri Avetisyan and Varsenik Khachatryan, "Nepotism at Schools in Armenia: A Cultural Perspective" (Edmond J. Safra Working Papers No. 51, Harvard University, 2014).
Zalpa, "'El que a buen árbol se arrima…'," 164-166.
Daniel Etounga-Manguelle, "Does Africa Need a Cultural Adjustment Program?" in Culture Matters: How Values Shape Human Progress, ed. Lawrence E. Harrison y Samuel P. Huntington (New York: Basic Books, 2000): 65-79, 75.
Adam Graycar and Tim Prenzler, Understanding and Preventing Corruption (Basingstoke: Palgrave Macmillan, 2013), doi: 10.1057/9781137335098.

Chapter 5

Lawrence E. Harrison, Jews, Confucians and Protestants: Cultural Capital and the End of Multiculturalism (Lanham: Rowman & Littlefield Publishers, 2013).
Lawrence E. Harrison and Samuel P. Huntington, ed. Culture Matters: How Values Shape Human Progress (New York: Basic Books, 2000), 13.
Katherine Marshall and Marisa Van Saanen, "Faith and Good Governance: Towards Strengthening Global Coalitions," (Berkley Center Reports, Berkley Center for Religion, Peace, and World Affairs, Washington, D.C.: 2009), 24, accessed 21 May 2018, https://s3.amazonaws.com/berkley-center/090117FaithGoodGovernanceTowardsStrengtheningGlobalCoalitions.pdf.
Alexander Jonathan Brown, "What is a National Integrity System: From Temple Blueprint to Hip-Pocket Guide," in Promoting Integrity: Evaluation and Improving Public Integrity Institutions, ed. Brian W. Head, Alexander Jonathan Brown, and Carmel Connors (Aldershot: Ashgate, 2008): 33-54, 45.
Séverine Deneulin and Carole Rakodi, "Revisiting Religion: Development Studies Thirty Years On," World Development Vol. 39:1 (2011): 45-54, 49, doi:10.1016/j.worlddev.2010.05.007.
Deneulin, "Revisiting Religion", 52.; Fukuyama, "Social Capital and Civil Society."; Justina Dugbazah, "The Relationships between Values, Religious Teaching and Development Concepts and Practices: A Preliminary Literature Review," (Religions and Development Research Programme Working Paper 33, University of Birmingham, 2009).
Pew Research Center, "Religion in Latin America: Widespread Change in a Historically Catholic Region," 13 November 2014. According to Pew Research's survey, "Christian" includes those who identify as Catholic, Protestant, Mormon, or Jehovah's Witness.
World Values Survey Wave 6 2010-2014 Official Aggregate v.20150418. World Values Survey Association (www.worldvaluessurvey.org). Aggregate File Producer: Asep/JDS, Madrid Spain, Questions V9, V25, V145, V152, available at http://www.worldvaluessurvey.org/WVSOnline.jsp.; World Values Survey Wave 5 2005-2008 Official Aggregate v.20140429. World Values Survey Association (www.worldvaluessurvey.org). Aggregate File Producer: Asep/JDS, Madrid Spain, Questions V188, V191, available at http://www.worldvaluessurvey.org/WVSOnline.jsp.
Gary A. Haugen, Good News about Injustice: A Witness of Courage in a Hurting World, (Downers Grove: InterVarsity Press, 2009).
Jeremiah 9:23-24; 22:15-16 (NKJV). Psalm 7:11; 11:5-7 (NKJV). Éxodus 22:26-27; Psalm 9:9,12; 12:5; Lamentations 3:36; James 5:4 (NKJV). Ezekiel 22:25-31 (NKJV). Isaiah 59:2-3, 15-16; Jeremiah 5:28-

29; 21:12; Amos 2:6-7; Zachariah 7:9-12; Luke 11:42 (NKJV).

Joel Edwards, “Corruption – A Biblical Reason to Respond,” (European Coalition of Apostolic Leaders, Nov 2013), accessed 21 May 2018, http://europeancoalitionofapostolicleaders.eu/read/article/351541.

Sidney E. Alhstrom, A Religious History of the American People (New Haven: Yale University Press, 1972), 637-640, cited in Gary A. Haugen, Good News about Injustice: A Witness of Courage in a Hurting World (Downers Grove: InterVarsity Press, 2009), 77.

Rafael La Porta, Florencio Lopez-de-Silanes, Andrei Shleifer, and Robert W. Vishnv, “The Quality of Government,” Journal of Law, Economics and Organization Vol. 15.1 (1999): 222-279, doi:10.1093/jleo/15.1.222.; David S. Landes, The Wealth and Poverty of Nations (New York: W.W. Norton, 1998).; Seymour Martin Lipset and Gabriel Salman Lenz, “Corruption, Culture and Markets,” in Culture Matters: How Values Shape Human Progress, ed. Lawrence E. Harrison and Samuel P. Huntington (New York: Basic Books, 2000): 112-124; Pellegrini, “Causes of Corruption.”; Robert D. Putnam, Making Democracy Work: Civic Traditions in Modern Italy (Princeton: Princeton University Press, 1993).; Treisman, “The Causes of Corruption”; Yaw M. Mensah, “An Analysis of the Effect of Culture and Religion on Perceived Corruption in a Global Context,” Journal of Business Ethics 121.2 (2014): 255-282, doi:10.1007/s10551-013-1696-0.

Treisman, “The Causes of Corruption,” 403, 427-428; Robert Dudley Woodberry and Timothy S. Shah, “The Pioneering Protestants,” Journal of Democracy Vol. 15.2 (2004): 47-61, 57, doi:10.1353/jod.2004.0037.

Chapter 6

Todd Michael Johnson, Kenneth R. Ross, and Sandra S. K. Lee, Atlas of Global Christianity 1910-2010 (Edinburgh: Edinburgh University Press, 2009).; Patrick J. StG Johnstone, Robyn Johnstone, and Jason Mandryk, Operation World (Carlisle/Waynesboro: Paternoster Lifestyle/Paternoster USA, 2001).

Robert Dudley Woodberry, “The Economic Consequences of Pentecostal Belief”, Society Vol.44.1 (2006): 29-35, 32, doi:10.1007/BF02690465.

Martin Allaby, Inequality, Corruption and the Church: Challenges and Opportunities in the Global Church (Eugene: Wipf and Stock Publishers, 2013).

Micah 3:11 (NKJV). Micah 6:10 (NKJV). Micah 7:3 (NKJV). Micah 7:5 (NKJV).

For more detail about methods for advocacy for integrity, see: Graham Gordon and Melissa Lawson, “Why advocate on governance and corruption?,” (Tearfund, 2012), accessed 21 May 2018, http://tilz.tearfund.org/~/media/Files/TILZ/Topics/Why_advocate_on_governance_and_corruption.pdf.

Joel Edwards and Geoff Tunnicliffe, “Micah Challenge International: A voice of evangelical advocacy,” Lausanne Global Analysis Vol. 4.2 (2015), accessed 21 May 2018, https://www.lausanne.org/content/lga/2015-03/micah-challenge-international; “Holy Hands? - Joel Edwards Calls the Church to Participate in a Global Campaign Against Corruption,” World Evangelical Alliance, 5 October 2012, accessed 21 May 2018, http://worldea.org/news/4097/holy-hands-joel-edwards-calls-the-church-to-participate-in-a-global-campaign-against-corruption; World Evangelical Alliance, “Anti-Corruption Campaign EXPOSED Launches.”

Quiénes Somos, Asociación para una Sociedad más Justa, 2015, accessed 21 May 2018, http://asjhonduras.com/webhn/sobre-nosotros/.

Yahya Wijaya, "Constructing an Anti-Corruption Theology," Exchange Vol 43.3 (2014): 221-236, 223-224, doi:10.1163/1572543X-12341325.

Marshall, "Faith and Good Governance," 25-26. Also see the resources available at: 13th International Anticorruption Conference, Athens, 30 October to 2 November 2008, accessed 21 May 2018, http://13iacc.org.s3-website.eu-central-1.amazonaws.com/index.html.

Christoph Stückelberger, "Corruption-Free Churches are Possible: Experiences, Values, Solutions," Globethics.net Focus Vol. 2, Geneva, 2010.

"Operation Nehemiah," Operation Nehemiah, n.d., accessed 21 May 2018, http://www.transitionnetwork.in/.; Arpit Waghmare, "Integrity and Anti-Corruption Case Study," Lausanne Movement video, 20 June 2013, accessed 21 May 2018, https://www.lausanne.org/content/integrity-and-anti-corruption-case-study-lausanne-global-leadership-forum.

Appendix 1

Transparency International, "Corruption Perceptions Index 2017," 21 February 2018, accessed 21 May 2018, https://www.transparency.org/research/cpi.

Todd M. Johnson and Gina A. Zurlo, eds. World Christian Database. Leiden/Boston: Brill. Accessed 21 May 2018.

World Bank, "Projects," accessed 21 May 2018, projects.worldbank.org.

USAID, "USAID Anticorruption Projects Database," accessed 21 May 2018, https://www.usaid.gov/data/dataset/b2cd92f6-e8bb-447b-9720-510222a80d0b.

Appendix 2

Hoge, D. R. (1972). A validated intrinsic religious motivation scale. Journal for the Scientific Study of Religion, 11, 369–376.

Regnum Mini-Books

Corruption and the Church | Martin Allaby
How do Christians in the global south see the relationship between the church and corruption? This book summarises the views of 101 leaders of churches, Christian faith-based organisations and anti-corruption organisations, as told during in-depth interviews with the author. Capturing voices from across three continents, this summary and analysis of their views makes for some uncomfortable reading, but suggests some constructive ways forward.

Deliver Us from Evil | Roberto Laver
Christians have been largely silent on the issue of corruption. Roberto Laver has been one of the few voices of the Christian community calling for the church to stand up and address this issue. Laver's scholarship undergirded by his faith and concern for the poor and marginalized, gives Christians a compelling wake-up call to confront this scourge. In so doing, he takes a big step toward filling a conspicuous gap in the literature of mission study and practice.

Confronting Corruption | Richard King
Corruption blights the lives of countless people around our world. The purpose of this book is to transform attitudes and behaviours of Christians who live in societies where corrupt behaviour is a fact of life and to do this by letting the Bible, as God's word, speak. The book is intended to be used for weekly reading by pastors at church services to remind congregations that corruption has no place in Christian life, as a resource for Bible colleges in training pastors/church workers and for small group Bible study.

Regnum Mini-Books

Unity & Reconciliation in Rwanda | S Cyuma
In the last ten years of the 20th century, the world was twice confronted with unbelievable news from Africa. Can we compare the situation in South Africa with that in Rwanda? Can Rwandan leaders draw lessons from the peace process in South Africa? These are some of the questions that this publication addresses.

Bridging the Cultural Gap | Ole Kirchheiner
This is an abridged version of Ole Kirchheiner's Regnum book, Culture and Christianity Negotiated in Hindu Society. Through an examination of the Nepali church the study pays special attention to the way ordinary Christians have been able to settle social and religious issues to live and work together with the traditional religious people of Nepal, and maintain a good family life.

Seeking Reconciliation | Peter Rowan
With a history of racial violence and in recent years, low-level ethnic tensions, the themes of peaceful coexistence and social harmony are recurring ones in the discourse of Malaysian society. In such a context, this book looks at the role of the church as a reconciling agent, arguing that a reconciling presence within a divided society necessitates an ethos of peacemaking. Such an ethos is created and sustained when Christians understand that their identity has been transformed in Jesus Christ.